First World War

and Army of Occupation

War Diary

France, Belgium and Germany

21 DIVISION
62 Infantry Brigade,
Brigade Machine Gun Company
23 February 1916 - 28 February 1918

WO95/2156/3

The Naval & Military Press Ltd
www.nmarchive.com
Published in association with The National Archives

Published by

The Naval & Military Press Ltd

Unit 10 Ridgewood Industrial Park,

Uckfield, East Sussex,

TN22 5QE England

Tel: +44 (0) 1825 749494

www.naval-military-press.com

www.nmarchive.com

This diary has been reprinted in facsimile from the original. Any imperfections are inevitably reproduced and the quality may fall short of modern type and cartographic standards.

Contents

Document type	Place/Title	Date From	Date To
Heading	WO95/2156-3		
Heading	62nd Machine Gun Coy. Feb 1916-Feb 1918		
War Diary	Grantham	23/02/1916	24/02/1916
War Diary	Southampton	24/02/1916	01/03/1916
War Diary	Havre	02/03/1916	02/03/1916
War Diary	Steinwerck	03/03/1916	03/03/1916
War Diary	Armentieres	04/03/1916	23/03/1916
War Diary	La Creche	23/03/1916	31/03/1916
War Diary	Longneau	31/03/1916	31/03/1916
War Diary	Cardonnette	01/04/1916	08/04/1916
War Diary	Bonnay	08/04/1916	15/04/1916
War Diary	Ville	15/04/1916	22/04/1916
War Diary	Meaulte	22/04/1916	02/05/1916
War Diary	Ville	03/05/1916	22/05/1916
War Diary	Meaulte	22/05/1916	29/05/1916
Miscellaneous	Cavalry Artillery And Infantry Only.	31/05/1916	31/05/1916
Heading	62nd Machine Gun Company. July 1916		
War Diary	Meaulte	01/07/1916	04/07/1916
War Diary	Dernancourt	04/07/1916	04/07/1916
War Diary	Ailly Sur Somme	04/07/1916	04/07/1916
War Diary	Argoeuves	05/07/1916	06/07/1916
War Diary	Preuill-Les-Molliens	06/07/1916	10/07/1916
War Diary	Corbie	10/07/1916	11/07/1916
War Diary	Mametz Wood	11/07/1916	11/07/1916
War Diary	Buire	18/07/1916	19/07/1916
War Diary	Dernancourt	20/07/1916	20/07/1916
War Diary	Saleux	21/07/1916	21/07/1916
War Diary	Dreuill-L-Molliens	22/07/1916	22/07/1916
War Diary	Pt Houvin	23/07/1916	23/07/1916
War Diary	Mazieres	23/07/1916	25/07/1916
War Diary	Manin	25/07/1916	27/07/1916
War Diary	Arras	28/07/1916	29/07/1916
Heading	62nd Brigade Machine Gun Company August 1916.		
War Diary	Arras	01/08/1916	30/08/1916
Miscellaneous	Appendix. 1. Orders By Cal. C.F. Dingwall. Commanding No 62 Co Machine Gun Corps.	01/08/1916	01/08/1916
Miscellaneous	Orders By Capt C.F. Dingwall Commanding 62 Co Machine Gun Corps.	07/08/1916	07/08/1916
Miscellaneous	Orders By Capt. C.F. Dingwall Commanding 62 Co. M.G.C.	08/08/1916	08/08/1916
Miscellaneous	Orders By Capt. C.F. Dingwall Commanding 62 Co. M.G.C. In The Field	08/08/1916	08/08/1916
Miscellaneous	Orders By Capt. G.G.N. Lodge Commanding 62 Co M.G.C.	14/08/1916	14/08/1916
Miscellaneous	Orders By Capt. G.G.N. Lodge Commanding 62 Co M.G.C.	15/08/1916	15/08/1916
Miscellaneous	Orders For Relief By Capt. G.G.N. Lodge	17/08/1916	17/08/1916
Miscellaneous	Orders By Capt. G.G.N. Lodge Commanding 62 Co. Machine Gun Corps.	19/08/1916	19/08/1916

Miscellaneous	Orders By Capt. G.G.N. Lodge. Commanding 62 Co Royal Machine Gun Corps. In The Field	26/08/1916	26/08/1916
Miscellaneous	Orders By Capt. G.G.N. Lodge. Commanding 62. Co. R.M.G.C. In The Field	26/08/1916	26/08/1916
Miscellaneous	Orders by Capt G.G.N. Lodge Commanding 62 Co. Royal Machine Gun Corps in the Field.	28/08/1916	28/08/1916
Heading	62nd Brigade Machine Gun Company September 1916.		
War Diary	Arras	01/09/1916	04/09/1916
War Diary	Grande Rullecourt	11/09/1916	14/09/1916
War Diary	Dernancourt	15/09/1916	16/09/1916
War Diary	Pommiers Redoubt	17/09/1916	17/09/1916
War Diary	Gueudecourt	18/09/1916	23/09/1916
War Diary	Fricourt Camp	24/09/1916	30/09/1916
War Diary	Near Trones Wood	01/10/1916	01/10/1916
War Diary	Buire	02/10/1916	03/10/1916
War Diary	Longpres	04/10/1916	04/10/1916
War Diary	Moufleurs	06/10/1916	08/10/1916
War Diary	Ladognoy	09/10/1916	09/10/1916
War Diary	Noeux-Le-Mines	10/10/1916	10/10/1916
War Diary	Vermelles	11/10/1916	26/12/1916
War Diary	Houchin	27/12/1916	27/12/1916
War Diary	Marles-Les-Mines	27/12/1916	31/12/1916
War Diary	Revillion	01/01/1917	27/01/1917
War Diary	Poperinghe	27/01/1917	27/01/1917
War Diary	Vox Vrie Farm	29/01/1917	15/02/1917
War Diary	Bethune	16/02/1917	16/02/1917
War Diary	Vermelles	16/02/1917	20/02/1917
War Diary	La Bourse	21/02/1917	28/02/1917
War Diary	Vox Vrie Farm	05/02/1917	13/02/1917
War Diary	Vermelles	17/02/1917	17/02/1917
War Diary	La Bourse	26/02/1917	28/02/1917
War Diary	Bethune	01/03/1917	01/03/1917
War Diary	Robeck	02/03/1917	02/03/1917
War Diary	La Miquellerie	03/03/1917	09/03/1917
War Diary	Ligny-Lez-Aire	10/03/1917	10/03/1917
War Diary	Bethonval	11/03/1917	11/03/1917
War Diary	Sericourt	12/03/1917	12/03/1917
War Diary	Halloy	13/03/1917	25/03/1917
War Diary	Bienvillers Au Bois	26/03/1917	27/03/1917
War Diary	Hamelincourt	29/03/1917	31/03/1917
War Diary	Croisilles	01/04/1917	02/04/1917
War Diary	Hamelincourt	04/04/1917	04/04/1917
War Diary	Hendecourt	05/04/1917	08/04/1917
War Diary	Boiry St Martin	09/04/1917	11/04/1917
War Diary	Boyelles	12/04/1917	15/04/1917
War Diary	Bretencourt	16/04/1917	24/04/1917
War Diary	Mercatel	26/04/1917	26/04/1917
War Diary	Boyelles	27/04/1917	30/04/1917
War Diary	NE St Leger	01/05/1917	04/05/1917
War Diary	Nr Henin	04/05/1917	12/05/1917
War Diary	Blairville	12/05/1917	19/05/1917
War Diary	Mercatel	19/05/1917	19/05/1917
War Diary	Blairville	19/05/1917	30/05/1917
War Diary	Railway Embankment	31/05/1917	31/05/1917
War Diary	Nr St Leger	01/06/1917	07/06/1917
War Diary	Moyenville	08/06/1917	18/06/1917

War Diary	Bailleulval	19/06/1917	29/06/1917
War Diary	Boyelles	30/06/1917	30/06/1917
War Diary	Hindernborgh Line	01/07/1917	02/07/1917
War Diary	Hinden Borgh Line H.Q.T.5.b.70.80	03/07/1917	16/07/1917
War Diary	Moyenville	16/07/1917	23/07/1917
War Diary	Hinden Borgh Line. HQ T5.b.80.75.	24/07/1917	27/07/1917
War Diary	Coy. H.Q. T5b 80.75	28/07/1917	30/07/1917
War Diary	Company H.Q. T5b.80.75.	30/07/1917	31/07/1917
War Diary	Hindenburgh Line Company H.Q. T.5.b.7980	01/08/1917	06/08/1917
War Diary	Hindenburgh Line Coy H.Q. T5.b.70.80	06/08/1917	09/08/1917
War Diary	E. Camp. Moyonville	10/08/1917	16/08/1917
War Diary	New Camp Moyonville	17/08/1917	25/08/1917
War Diary	N Moyonville	25/08/1917	27/08/1917
War Diary	Moyenville	28/08/1917	28/08/1917
War Diary	Dainville	29/08/1917	08/09/1917
War Diary	Dickebush	09/09/1917	18/09/1917
War Diary	In The Line	19/09/1917	23/09/1917
War Diary	Meteren	23/09/1917	28/09/1917
War Diary	Conqueror Camp Westoutre	29/09/1917	29/09/1917
War Diary	Westoutre & Scottish Wood	30/09/1917	30/09/1917
Operation(al) Order(s)	62nd Machine Gun Company. Operation Order No. 1/17. Appendix A	17/09/1917	17/09/1917
War Diary	Scottish Wood Near Dickebush	01/10/1917	02/10/1917
War Diary	Coy. HQ. In The Line.	03/10/1917	04/10/1917
War Diary	Polygon Wood	05/10/1917	07/10/1917
War Diary	Camp (Scottish Wood)	08/10/1917	09/10/1917
War Diary	Wallon Capelle	10/10/1917	19/10/1917
War Diary	Dickebush	20/10/1917	21/10/1917
War Diary	In The Line (E Of Polygon Wood)	22/10/1917	29/10/1917
War Diary	Scottish Wood (Anzac Camp)	30/10/1917	31/10/1917
Operation(al) Order(s)	62 Machine Gun Coy. Report on Operations in connection with the attack on 4th October 1917	12/10/1917	12/10/1917
Miscellaneous	62nd Coy. Machine Gun Corps.		
War Diary	Anzac Camp. Dickebush Area	01/11/1917	05/11/1917
War Diary	Anzac Camp & In The Line	05/11/1917	05/11/1917
War Diary	In The Line	06/11/1917	15/11/1917
War Diary	Westoutre	16/11/1917	17/11/1917
War Diary	Vieux Berquin Area (West.)	17/11/1917	18/11/1917
War Diary	Busnes Area (East)	18/11/1917	18/11/1917
War Diary	Busnes Area Barlin	19/11/1917	19/11/1917
War Diary	St. Eloi	20/11/1917	20/11/1917
War Diary	Maroeuil	21/11/1917	30/11/1917
Operation(al) Order(s)	32 Machine Gun Company Operation Order No. 111. Appendix "A".		
Miscellaneous	Appendices.		
Miscellaneous	62nd Company-Machine Gun Compy. Appendix-B		
Miscellaneous	62 Coy. Machine Gun Corps. Appendix C	26/11/1917	26/11/1917
War Diary	Peronne	01/12/1917	01/12/1917
War Diary	Cartigny	02/12/1917	03/12/1917
War Diary	Longuevesnes	04/12/1917	09/12/1917
War Diary	In The Line	10/12/1917	14/12/1917
War Diary	In The Field	15/12/1917	18/12/1917
War Diary	Heudecourt	19/12/1917	25/12/1917
War Diary	In The Line	26/12/1917	31/12/1917
Miscellaneous	62nd Machine Gun Company. Monthly Report For Month Ending 20/12/17.		

Operation(al) Order(s)	62nd Coy. M.G. Corps Operation Order No. 122.	17/12/1917	17/12/1917
Miscellaneous	Appendix To Provisional Machine Gun Scheme Submitted 3-12-17.	04/12/1917	04/12/1917
Miscellaneous	Ref. Map Sheets. 57c. S.E. R 62c. N.E.	03/12/1917	03/12/1917
Operation(al) Order(s)	62nd M.G. Coy. Operation Order No. 90.	09/12/1917	09/12/1917
Operation(al) Order(s)	62 Machine Gun Coy. Operation Order No. 221.		
Operation(al) Order(s)	62nd Machine Gun Company. Operation Order No. 251.		
Map	Appendix 2		
War Diary	In The Field	01/01/1918	03/01/1918
War Diary	Heudecourt	04/01/1918	11/01/1918
War Diary	In The Line	12/01/1918	20/01/1918
War Diary	Heaudecourt	20/01/1918	28/01/1918
War Diary	Heaudecourt In The Line	29/01/1918	31/01/1918
War Diary	Heaudecourt	01/02/1918	02/02/1918
War Diary	Haut Allaines	03/02/1918	14/02/1918
War Diary	Tincourt	15/02/1918	26/02/1918
War Diary	Ronssoy	27/02/1918	28/02/1918
Operation(al) Order(s)	O.O. No. J. 30.	30/01/1918	30/01/1918
Operation(al) Order(s)	62 Machine Gun Coy. Operation Orders No. 26.	26/01/1918	26/01/1918
Operation(al) Order(s)	62 Machine Gun Coy. Operation Order No. J. 21.	21/01/1918	21/01/1918
Operation(al) Order(s)	62nd Machine Gun Coy O.O. 301.	18/01/1918	18/01/1918
Operation(al) Order(s) Miscellaneous	62nd Machine Gun Coy. Operations Order No. 101.		
Operation(al) Order(s)	62nd Company Machine Gun Corps. Operation Orders 1.1	01/01/1918	01/01/1918
Miscellaneous	62 Machine Gun Coy.	19/01/1918	19/01/1918

21ST DIVISION
62ND INFY BDE

62ND MACHINE GUN COY.

FEB 1916 - FEB 1918

Instructions regarding War Diaries and Intelligence Summaries are contained in F. S. Regs., Part II. and the Staff Manual respectively. Title pages will be prepared in manuscript.

WAR DIARY

or

~~INTELLIGENCE SUMMARY.~~

(Erase heading not required.)

Army Form C. 2118.

~~XXI~~ Vol 1+2

62 Machine Gun Company. Vol 2

Machine Gun Corps.

Place	Date	Hour	Summary of Events and Information	Remarks and references to Appendices
GRANTHAM	23/2/16	Midnight	Marched out of camp with Company complete for Front.	
"	24/2/16	1 A.M.	Train left GRANTHAM STATION for SOUTHAMPTON.	
SOUTHAMPTON	24/2/16	10.30 a.m.	Arrive SOUTHAMPTON and remained on wharf.	
		4.30 p.m.	Embarked on S.S. AUSTRALIND, except 3 Officers 55 N.C.O's and men who at same time embarked on S.S. MARGUERITA and went across to HAVRE in the night and stayed in Rest Camp there till the arrival of remainder of Company.	
	24/2/16 to 1/3/16		Lay in SOUTHAMPTON WATER waiting for favourable opportunity to cross.	
HAVRE	2/3/16	3 a.m.	Arrived in HAVRE ROADS & lay there till about 8 a.m. when we drew up to wharf and disembarked	
		12.30 p.m.	Completed disembarking and remained on wharf during the afternoon. The remainder of Company join us about 3 p.m. Drew all our winter clothing, etc	
		6.30 p.m.	March to Point 3 and entrain.	
		10.30 p.m.	Train starts.	
STEINWERCK	3/3/16	8.30 p.m.	Arrive at Railhead at STEINWERCK and detrain	
		10.30 p.m.	Detrainment complete ~~start~~ to march to billets at ARMENTIÈRES	
ARMENTIÈRES	4/3/16	1 A.M.	Arrive at our billets at ARMENTIÈRES	
"	4/3/16	5 p.m.	Go up to trenches — 12 guns up in Subsidiary Line and Support Points.	

T2134. Wt. W708–776. 500000. 4/15. Sir J. C. & S.

Instructions regarding War Diaries and Intelligence Summaries are contained in F. S. Regs., Part II. and the Staff Manual respectively. Title pages will be prepared in manuscript.

WAR DIARY
or
~~INTELLIGENCE SUMMARY.~~
(Erase heading not required.)

Army Form C. 2118.

62 Machine Gun Company
Machine Gun Corps.

Place	Date	Hour	Summary of Events and Information	Remarks and references to Appendices
ARMENTIÈRES	17/3/16	night	Relieved by 64 M.G. Coy. and returned to billets in ARMENTIÈRES. During this first stay in the trenches no firing of any kind was done	
	19/3/16		Inspected by the G.O.C. 62 Inf. Bde.	
	13/3/16 to 21/3/16	night	Go up to trenches with 16 guns taking over 4 additional emplacements from 63 M.G. Coy. on the right. During the period from 13th – 21st indirect fire at night was applied almost every night at enemy trenches railways and dumps etc. During the time in trenches we strengthened the emplacements and built several additional and alternative emplacements.	
	22/3/16		Division relieved. Handed over to and relieved by 52 M.G. Coy. spent the night in billets at ARMENTIÈRES. Division moving out to Rest.	
	23/3/16	5.30AM	Start to march to LA CRÈCHE billeting area.	
LA CRÈCHE	23/3/16	3 p.m.	Arrive at LA CRÈCHE. During the stay in this area training of every branch was carried out.	
	25/3/16		Inspected by Commander-in-Chief of the British Army - Sir Douglas Haig – (without transport)	
	28/3/16		Inspected by Commander-in-Chief Second Army – (with transport)	
	31/3/16	1AM	March from LA CRÈCHE to GODEWAERSVELDE arriving there at 8 a.m. entrained for LONGNEAU.	
LONGNEAU	31/3/16	11 p.m.	Arrive at LONGNEAU and start to march to billets at CARDONNETTE.	

T2134. Wt. W708–776. 500000. 4/15. Sir J. C. & S.

Instructions regarding War Diaries and Intelligence Summaries are contained in F. S. Regs., Part II. and the Staff Manual respectively. Title pages will be prepared in manuscript.

WAR DIARY
or
~~INTELLIGENCE~~ SUMMARY.
(Erase heading not required.)

Army Form C. 2118.

62 Machine Gun Company
Machine Gun Corps.

Place	Date	Hour	Summary of Events and Information	Remarks and references to Appendices
CARDONNETTE	1/4/16	2 A.M	Arrive at billets at CARDONNETTE. Training carried on	
	4/4/16		G.O.C 62 Inf. Bde. approves of 8 men from each Batt[n] being attached to company. This gives 32 more men - Their training in machine gun work is started at once and continued during the whole period at Rest.	
	8/4/16	9 A.M.	March from CARDONNETTE to billets at BONNAY arriving there about midday.	
BONNAY.	8/4/16 to 15/4/16		Stay at BONNAY - Training carried on systematically all the time here —	
	15/4/16	9 a.m.	March to VILLE.	
VILLE	15/4/16	11 a.m.	Arrive at billets at Ville. 1st reinforcement arrived (1 man)	
	15/4/16 to 22/4/16		Stay at VILLE. Training again carried on. During this time new attached men have progressed satisfactorily with training and are put through Part I. Table C. and a modified part of Part II Table C. — 2nd reinforcement arrived (1 man)	
MÈAULTE	22/4/16	9 a.m.	Move to trenches near MÈAULTE. Coy H.qrs at MÈAULTE. Take over emplacements from 63 M.G. Coy. 13 guns in trenches, 3 in reserve at MÈAULTE.	
MÈAULTE.	27/4/16		3rd reinforcement arrived (2 men)	

[illegible signature]
Capt.
O.C. 62 M. G. Coy.
M. G. Corps

27/4/16.

T2134. Wt. W708-776. 500000. 4/15. Sir J. C. & S.

Instructions regarding War Diaries and Intelligence Summaries are contained in F. S. Regs., Part II. and the Staff Manual respectively. Title pages will be prepared in manuscript.

WAR DIARY
or
~~INTELLIGENCE SUMMARY.~~
(Erase heading not required.)

XX1 Army Form C. 2118.

62 Machine Gun Coy. Vol 3

Place	Date	Hour	Summary of Events and Information	Remarks and references to Appendices
Meaulte	2/5/16	7 am	Relieved by 64 M G Coy. & proceed to VILLE.	
VILLE	3/5/16.		March to billets at LA NEUVILLE.	
	13/5/16	9 am	March to reserve in billets at VILLE.	
VILLE.	22/5/16		Relieve 63 M G Coy in trenches before MEAULTE. Coy H'qrs at MEAULTE.	
MEAULTE.	22/29/5/16. 5/16.		During this stay in trenches activity on either side normal, nothing calling for special comment.	

[signature] Maj.
Comdg 62 M G Coy
M G Corps.

T2134. Wt. W708–776. 500000. 4/15. Sir J. C. & S.

To be rendered to Officers i/c Records for transmission to the War Office.

Army Form B. 158.

CAVALRY, ARTILLERY and INFANTRY only.

Regiment, etc., or Depot No 62 Coy. Machine Gun Corps

Station In the Field

Date 31/5/16.

LIST OF OFFICERS.

* Married or Single.	Officers doing duty with the Unit. NAME.		Date of being taken on the strength of the Unit.†	Stations (if on Detachment).
	Lieut.-Colonel—			
S	Majors—	J. H. Mc Innes Skinner		
	Captains—			
M	Lieutenants—	F. C. Swallow.		
S		H. W. Edwardes.		
S	2nd Lieutenants—	M. Smithers		
S		T. J. B. Troman.		
M		W. D. Colley.		
M		J. Dodson		
M		C. J. Colley.		
	Adjutant—			
	Quartermaster—			
	Riding Master—			

WARRANT OFFICERS.

Master Gunner—

Coy. Serjeant-Major— Galletly. H.

Bandmaster—

OFFICERS ATTACHED.

(Including Special Reserve and Territorial Force Officers. Authority to be quoted.)

Rank.	Name.	Corps.	Authority.	Date of joining.

* The letter "M" or "S" is to be placed before the names of Officers.
† For Units of Royal Artillery, Depots of all Arms and Special Reserve Units.
NOTE.—The word "Sick" to be inserted against the names of all Officers who are on the Sick List, and the words "Assistant Adjutant," "Instructor of Gunnery," &c., against the name of an Officer holding such appointment.

(4358) Wt. 9246—1807. 350,000. 12/14. J. T. & S., Ltd. Forms B. 158 / 7

Officers absent on duty.

(Exclusive of seconded Officers, but including Officers posted and not joined.)

Married or Single.	Rank and Name.	On what duty, at what station, from what time.

Officers and Warrant Officers absent with Leave.

	Rank and Name.	By whose permission, and date of order.	On what account.	From what time.	To what time.

Officers and Warrant Officers who have *joined* during the preceding month, showing whether from leave of absence, on appointment, &c.

	Rank and Name.	Date and cause.

Officers and Warrant Officers who have *quitted* during the preceding month, showing whether on leave of absence, removal, death, &c.

	Rank and Name.	Date and cause.
S	2/Lt W. L. Bonny	Evacuated to England suffering from Dilated heart caused by Shell Shock.

Officers absent without leave.

Rank and Name.	Since what time.

W. G. Edwards Lieut & Adjt for Maj Commanding.

62 M. G. Coy

62nd Inf.Bde.
21st Div.

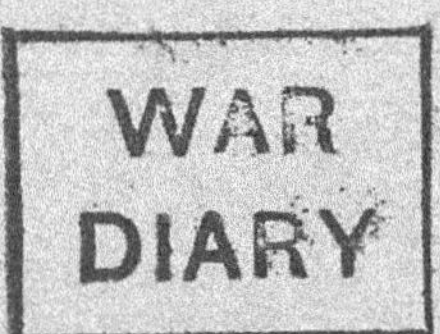

62nd MACHINE GUN COMPANY.

J U L Y

1 9 1 6

I

3 Sheets

Army Form C. 2118.

62 M. G. Coy.

Instructions regarding War Diaries and Intelligence Summaries are contained in F. S. Regs., Part II. and the Staff Manual respectively. Title pages will be prepared in manuscript.

WAR DIARY
or
~~INTELLIGENCE SUMMARY.~~

(Erase heading not required.)

Place	Date	Hour	Summary of Events and Information	Remarks and references to Appendices
Méaulte	1/7/16		Company in reserve at QUEENS REDOUBT in trenches near Méaulte	
	1/7/16	6 p.m.	2 Sections with 8 guns moved up to SUNKEN Rd in front of CRUCIFIX TRENCH. 3 Casualties	
	2/7/16	12.30 a.m.	Took up positions in SUNKEN Rd relieving 64 M G Company. Two casualties by SHELL FIRE	
	2/7/16	6.30 p.m.	Remaining 2 sections moved up to SUNKEN Rd	
	3/7/16	8.30 a.m.	Indirect fire employed with three guns during bombardment on the ground between SHELTER WOOD and BOTTOM WOOD.	
		9.30 a.m.	6 guns advanced to CRUCIFIX TRENCH on the left, 4 guns took up positions in SHELTER WOOD 4 guns took up positions in CRUCIFIX TRENCH on the right of SHELTER WOOD 2 guns kept in reserve. 12 Casualties 10 wounded 2 killed	
	4/7/16	6.0 a.m.	Relieved by 52 M G COMPANY marched to DERNANCOURT	
DERNANCOURT		6.0 p.m.	Entrained for AILLY-SUR-SOMME LIEUT DICKSON and 2/LIEUT WALKER joined for duty.	
AILLY SUR SOMME		11 p.m.	Detrained and marched to ARGOEUVES into billets.	
ARGOEUVES	5/7/16	5.30 p.m.	Reinforcements arrived 32 men	
	6/7/16		Marched to DREUIL-LES-MOLLIENS.	
DREUIL-LES-MOLLIENS	8/7/16	12.30 p.m.	2/LIEUT. YATES joined for duty	
	11/7/16	5.30 a.m.	Marched to AILLY-SUR-SOMME entrained for CORBIE.	

T2134. Wt. W708–776. 500000. 4/15. Sir J. C. & S.

II

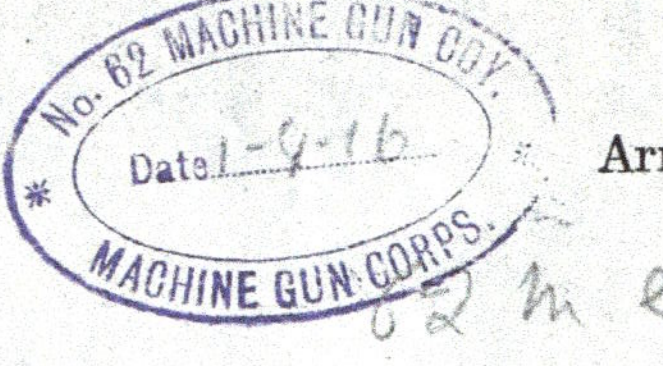

62 M. G. Coy

Army Form C. 2118.

Instructions regarding War Diaries and Intelligence Summaries are contained in F. S. Regs., Part II. and the Staff Manual respectively. Title pages will be prepared in manuscript.

WAR DIARY
or
~~INTELLIGENCE SUMMARY.~~

(Erase heading not required.)

Place	Date	Hour	Summary of Events and Information	Remarks and references to Appendices
CORBIE	10/7/16	11.30pm	Marched into billets at MÉAULTE.	
"	11/7/16	10pm	Marched into trenches in MAMETZ WOOD in support line, 12 guns in trenches 4 in reserve.	
MAMETZ WOOD	11/7/16 to 18/7/16		In support trenches in MAMETZ WOOD, 4 guns put out of action. 40 casualties 8 killed 32 wounded.	
~~MAMETZ WOOD~~ BUIRE	18/7/16	4.30am	Relieved by 100 M.G. COMPANY marched into billets at BUIRE. 10 men joined for duty.	
"	19/7/16	4.30pm	35 men joined for duty. Guns thoroughly overhauled and cleaned. 4 new guns arrived.	
DERNANCOURT	20/7/16	5.30pm	Entrained for SALEUX.	
SALEUX	21/7/16	1am.	Detrained and marched into billets at DREUILL-LES-MOLLIENS.	
DREUILL-L-MOLLIENS	22/7/16	5.30am	Marched to OISSY went by motor bus to RIFLE RANGE AMIENS. Marched to LONGUEAU and entrained for Pt. HOUVIN.	
Pt. HOUVIN	23/7/16	4.30am	Detrained and marched into billets at MAZIÈRES	
MAZIÈRES	23/7/16 to 24/7/16		In billets at MAZIÈRES.	
"	25/7/16	5.30pm	Marched into billets at MANIN.	
MANIN.	25/7/16 - 27/7/16		Machine gun Drill & gas helmet Drill. Capt C.F. Dingwall joined & took over command.	
"	27/7/16	9.30	Went by motor bus to WANQUETIN and marched to ARRAS.	
ARRAS.	28/7/16	5.30am.	Relieved 43 M.G. COMPANY in trenches near ARRAS, five guns in trenches 10 in reserve at Headquarters in ARRAS. (1 gun deficient.)	

T2134. Wt. W708–776. 500000. 4/15. Sir J. C. & S.

Instructions regarding War Diaries and Intelligence Summaries are contained in F. S. Regs., Part II. and the Staff Manual respectively. Title pages will be prepared in manuscript.

WAR DIARY
or
INTELLIGENCE SUMMARY.

(Erase heading not required.)

Army Form C. 2118.

III

62 M. G. Coy

Place	Date	Hour	Summary of Events and Information	Remarks and references to Appendices
ARRAS.	28/7/16 – 31/7/16		On trenches near ARRAS two emplacements taken over in I Sector, 6 guns in trenches & in reserve (1 gun deficient) at Headquarters.	
	29/7/16	6.30 pm	2LTS W.R. TIPTAFT – J.B. BROWN – J. BOSWELL joined the company.	

C F Swinfell
Captain.
O. C. "62" Coy., Machine Gun Corps.

T2134. Wt. W708–776. 500000. 4/15. Sir J. C. & S.

62nd Brigade.

21st Division.

62nd BRIGADE MACHINE GUN COMPANY

AUGUST 1916.

VOL 6 3 pages 62 MGC

Army Form C. 2118.

WAR DIARY
or
INTELLIGENCE SUMMARY.
(Erase heading not required.)

Instructions regarding War Diaries and Intelligence Summaries are contained in F. S. Regs., Part II. and the Staff Manual respectively. Title pages will be prepared in manuscript.

Place	Date	Hour	Summary of Events and Information	Remarks and references to Appendices
ARRAS	1/8/16		No 4949 Cpl GARSIDE receives the DCM for gallantry in the Field	1
"	2/8/16	7.30am	No 1 Section relieved No 4 Section in J TRENCHES.	1
			No ~~4~~ Subsection relieved No 3 Sub section in J TRENCHES	1
			No 6 Subsection took over new emplacement	1
			~~Three~~ Seven guns in the line ~~six~~ nine in reserve.	
ARRAS	8/8/16	7.30am	No 4 Section relieved No 1, No 3 sub relieved No 6 subsection	2
			No 5 subsection relieved 4 Subsection in I Sector	
			eight guns in line, three guns in ~~support~~ support and five guns in reserve in ARRAS. Guns swept enemy parapet at intervals during the night.	2
ARRAS	11/8/16		Cpl Copeman L/Cpl Hope L/Cpl May Pte Reilly proceeded to CAMIERS for an advanced course of Machine gun (VICKERS)	
ARRAS	12/8/16		CAPT G.G. ~~S.A.~~ N. LODGE 2nd East Surrey took over command - CAPT C F DINGWALL 3rd EAST SURREYS appointed second in command.	
			2nd Lt J DODSON appointed in command of No 2 SECTION - 2nd Lt YATES in command of No 1 SECTION	4
			L/Cpl BROMLEY who died of wounds at the base, got the Military Medal	4

Army Form C. 2118.

WAR DIARY
or
INTELLIGENCE SUMMARY.
(Erase heading not required.)

Instructions regarding War Diaries and Intelligence Summaries are contained in F. S. Regs., Part II. and the Staff Manual respectively. Title pages will be prepared in manuscript.

Place	Date	Hour	Summary of Events and Information	Remarks and references to Appendices
ARRAS	15/8/16	9.15	No 1 Section relieved No 4 Section	5
			No 6 Subsection " No 3 Sub "	"
			No 4 Subsection " No 5 " "	"
			All officers read confidential and secret memos up to date	"
			Pte GOULAND went for a course of cooking at Third ARMY HQ's	"
"	18/8/16		The 62nd Coy Royal Machine Gun Corps relieved the 18th Batty M M G (4 guns) and 33rd Coy Royal Machine Gun Corps in I Rt. The 62 Coy were relieved by the 110th Coy in J Sector and two guns in I	6
			No 2 Section relieved M M G (4 guns)	"
			No 1 Section relieved 2 guns of 33rd Coy and also two unoccupied emplacements. 8 guns in line	"
			A company canteen started two branches in trenches and one at HQs in ARRAS.	7
	21/8/16		2 more guns of No 3 section put in line	
	22/8/16		Positions prepared for night firing — until this night firing was withheld for tactical reasons.	

Instructions regarding War Diaries and Intelligence Summaries are contained in F. S. Regs., Part II. and the Staff Manual respectively. Title pages will be prepared in manuscript.

WAR DIARY
or
INTELLIGENCE SUMMARY.
(Erase heading not required.)

Army Form C. 2118.

Place	Date	Hour	Summary of Events and Information	Remarks and references to Appendices
ARRAS	21/8/16		Sgt WHITEHEAD returned from leave from England.	
"	23/8/16		Sgt GUNN and Corpl ANDERSON left for leave in England	
"	24/8/16		On receipt of WAR OFFICE LETTER dated 8 August No 16/Eastern/494 Accounts 2 it is noted that the corps is now the ROYAL MACHINE GUN CORPS.	
			NIGHT FIRING was carried out especially on 1 FREDS WOOD 2) Wood NW of FREDS WOOD, south of river only.	
"	26/8/16		COPY OF COMPANY ORDERS attached PART I & II	8
			5 supernumerary L/Cpls appointed. Lt WARREN left the company sick	
"	28/8/16		NIGHT FIRING ON CAMBRAI ROAD	
"	29/8/16		No 4 Section relieved No 1 Section	9
			12 guns in line 4 in reserve	
	30/8/16		Collection for LORD KITCHENER'S memorial amounted to over eighty francs	9

[signature] Capt

Comdg 62 Coy Royal Machine Gun Corps.
31/8/16

Appendix. 1.

Orders by. Capt. C. F. ... Dingwall.
Commanding No 62 Co Machine Gun Corps.

In the field.

1.8.16.

I. Divisional General Routine Order is reproduced. In the first line Trenches every N.C.O and man will always have his rifle with him on whatever duty he is employed.

Divisional Routine Order 568. 570.

II. Steel Helmets will always be worn by all troops in Arras and Environs

III Commander in Chief has awarded the D.C.M. to 4949 Cpl. Garside. He receives congratulations from Staff & Company.

2nd Lt. Tiptaft and No 1 Section will take over Trenches from No 4. Section to-morrow. They will move off by 8.0am. Report by Phone when relief is complete. This Officer will arrange to take up Telephone Orderly and Runner. Nominal Roll of Gun Teams to be submitted to Co. H Qrs by 8.0am.

IV 2nd Lt. Brown of No 4 Sub Section will take over from Mr Yates to-morrow at 8.0am. Telephone Orderly and runner will remain. Report by Phone when relief is complete.

V Attention to all Officers is drawn to Corps & Divisional Orders to be found in C. H. Qtrs. The Commanding Officer is dissatisfied with the way in which Trench Work is carried out. Far more care must be taken of the gun ammunition and Trench Stores. All must be cleaned daily.

VI Officers taking over Trenches are to read Commanding Officers Signal Book before to-morrow morning 8.0 am.

VII 2nd Lt. Boswell and one Gun Team from No 6. Sub. Section will take over emplacement. Which will be shown by C.O. at 8.30 am. to-morrow morning. It will be notified to-morrow morning if hand carts are available.

VIII Teams will take up their own filled Belt Boxes to-morrow morning.

2

Aug 7th 16.

Orders by Capt. C F Dingwall
Commanding 62 Co. Machine Gun Corp.

1 Reliefs will take place tomorrow.

2 Gun teams will leave H. Qtrs at 7.30 am.

3 Hand carts will if possible be arranged for.

4. No 4 Section will relieve No 1 Section. No 3 Sub Section relieve No 6 Sub Section

5 No 4 Section will take up with them 1 Section Cook 1 Orderly 1 Telephone Orderly

6 No 5. Sub Section will take up 2 guns of No 3 Sub. Section now in the CASERNE to I Section and relieve No 4. Sub. Section.

7. No 3. Sub Section will take No 5. Sub Sections guns now in 2nd Lieut Boswells' dugout. There are 5 Belt Boxes there, also to each gun also 2 spare parts case.

8. No 5 Subsection will take 1 Cook. 1 Orderly and one Telephone operator.

9. Relieving Officers will take over all trench stores alloted to each gun position and sign for them.

Cont.

10. All necessary Coy. Trench Stores such as Periscopes, Very Pistols, etc. also to be handed over & signed for. Relief Officer to bring down duplicate copy of each handing over statement.

11. Reference Order 4.

One team of No. 3. Sub Section will relieve the team of No. 1 in May Avenue, and one team of No. 4 Section to relieve the team of No. 6 Subsection in RUSSIAN SAP.

12 All relieved teams belt boxes to be brought back with ammunition.

13 No. 1 Section will leave two guns, two tripods, and two spare part cases in Officer dug-out Oil Work. They must be thoroughly cleaned before putting in VICKERS CHESTS at Officer dug-out which belong to No. 5 Sub Section.

14 There will be no ration parties to-night.

C. F. Dingwall Capt.

Com. 62 Co. M. G. C.

Orders by Capt C. F. Dingwall
Commanding 62 Co. M. G. C
In the field.

Aug 8th 16

Orderly Officer 2nd Lt Brown

I. Guns and ammunition to be thoroughly cleaned.

II. Rifle and equipment inspection at 2.0 pm.
Gas Helmets will also be inspected on this parade.

III. Indents for deficiencies should be submitted by 4.0 pm. to day.

C.F. Dingwall Capt
Com 62 Co M. G. C

Orders by Capt. G. N. Lodge Cmdg 62 Co M.G.C.

Company Orderly Officer 2nd Lt Brown
Next for duty 2nd Tipper

Orders for company orderly Officer will be found in Orderly Room.

Posting. 2nd Lt Dodes is posted in command of No 2 Sec. from to day inclusive. 2nd Lt Yates to Command No 1 Section. Lt Yates will not take over command till relief takes place.

Posting. L/Cpl. Foster is appointed acting sanitary Corporal in addition to post corporal. He will receive daily instructions from the C.S.M. as to his duties

Steel Helmets.

G.R.O. is again republished for information & immediate action. All ranks will wear Steel Helmets on all occasions in Arras and its Environs. Section Officers will return to the storeman all caps correctly marked inside with the name and number of the owner in sacks by 10 pm 13.8.16 A list of deficiencies will be sent to O.R at same time.

Range Card Boards.

New range card boards are being sent out this evening. If old boards are illegible the new boards must be used. Boards that are not wanted to be returned.

Letters Censoring of

The orderly Officer will censor all Hd Qrs Staff Letters. All Letters to be ready for censor-ship at 10.o/p the orderly Officer will bring them up to O.R by that time.

Church of England.

Voluntary services will be held as follows

Soldiers Club.

Holy Communion 7.30a

Evening Service 9.30a

Parade.

Section Officers will inspect their Section every morning 9.30a

Death.

The Commanding Officer regrets to announce the death of L Cpl. Bramley who had gained M.M

C F Dingwall Capt.

62. Co M.G.C.

~~8~~ 5

Orders by Capt. P G N Lodge
commanding 62 Co M.G.C.

In the field

14.8.16.

1. Relief will take place tomorrow. Gun teams will leave headquarters 7.15 am. Hand carts have been arranged for.

2. No. 1. Section under 2nd Lieut Tiptaft will relieve No. 4. Section.
No 6. Sub section " " " Boswell " " No 3 Sub "
No 4 " " " " " Dodson " " No 5 Sub ".

3. 2nd Lieut Tiptaft will take two guns tripods etc etc from CASERNE and the two guns now in / Officer dugout, also 30 filled belt boxes, ten more will be found in / Officers dugout.

4. 2nd Lieut Boswell will take up one gun tripod etc etc, 10 filled belt boxes and take the gun etc etc in MGRE ~~dug~~ DOUBT. dugout.

5. 2nd Lieut Dodson will take two guns tripods etc etc & 20 filled belt boxes.

6. A Fatigue Party under Sgt Goodly will take up one gun tripod spare part case etc etc of No. 6 Sub section and 10 filled belt boxes. to M.G. Redoubt to-night. and bring away the gun tripod spare parts case etc, and the five belt boxes now there belonging to No. 4 Sub section.

7. Lieut Dickson will clean thoroughly and leave two guns tripods etc etc 20 Belt boxes in / Officer dugout.

8. Officers will hand over a separate list all company Trench Stores such as Periscopes Very Pistols as the company has not yet full complement of these stores

9 All tripods to be changed this relief.

14.8.16.

10. Cooks detailed elsewhere will return tonight.

11. Officers are reminded to check all trench stores stationery in company before signing

12. One gun etc of No 5 Sub section will be taken up to M.G. Redoubt tomorrow afternoon.

13. On completion of relief. wire "Done"
Normal roll of gun teams, orderlies etc can be seen at Headquarters.

14. Breakfast for relieving teams will be in Barrack at 6.15 a.m. before starting. Breakfast for relieved teams on returning to barrack. No ration parties tonight: Baths have been arranged for relieved teams

15. Orderly Officer tomorrow. 2nd Lt Brown.
next for duty. Lt Dickson.

The orderly officer will inspect all breakfasts and dinners in barrack tomorrow.

16. 2nd Lt Tiptaft will take up two Vickers Chests of No 4 Section and Lt Dickson will bring down the two chests now there belonging to No 5 Sub section

17. Relieving Officers will read certain confidential news on Secret Orders at ~~[illegible]~~ 9.15 tonight at Hd. Qtrs.

C. F. Dingwall

Captain.
[illegible] Coy., Machine Gun Corps.

5a

Orders by Capt G. G. N. Lodge
Commanding 62 Co M.G.C. 15.8.16

1. Orderly Officer.

Orderly Officer tomorrow Lt Dickson
Next for duty 2nd " Yates

2 Section Renumbering of

In future the Sub-Sections of No. 1 Section will be known as 1A. 1B
" - - - - - - - - - - - - - - 2A. 2B
" - - - - - - - - - - - - - - 3A. 3B
- - - - - - - - - - - - - - - 4A. 4B

3. Post Loss of

It is notified for information that one bag of mails belonging to the company was lost in a railway accident on the 10th of August most probably posted in England on the 7th or 8th.

4. Cap Return of.

Reference Coy order Steel Helmets 12 8 16
Teams that have returned from trenches today will hand in to store by 8.0a tomorrow all caps packed in a sack without fail. Authority C.R.O. 1099

5 Clothing Change of Clothing.

Section Officers will parade at the undermentioned times tomorrow all men wanting change of clothing.

No 4. 10.am No 2B. 10.15am No 3A 10.30am

Discipline. 2nd Lt Yates will hand over 2B to 2nd Lt Brown tomorrow

C F Dingwall Capt & Adjt

Orders for relief by 6 Secret

Capt. G. G. N. Lodge

Commanding 62 Co M. G. Co 17.8.16

1 The 62nd Machine Gun Co will relieve the 18th MMG and the 33rd M. G. Co in I Sector on the afternoon of the 18th.

2. This sector will be divided up into two Sub Sectors I Right and I Left Boundary Line Infantry. Line.

3 No 2. Section will relieve the 4 Guns of the 18th M. M. G. B. in I Left and they will meet guides for these positions at the Railway Station at 2 op.

4. No 1 Section will relieve 2 guns of the 33rd M. G. Co in I Right and will also occupy two positions, which are at present not used. Two guides from 33rd M. G. Co will be at 62nd Hd Qtrs at 1.45 p for 2 positions. 2nd Lt Boswell will act as guide for the position he was shown. 2nd Lt. Tiplaft knows the fourth position.

5 One hand cart and carrying party will be provided for No 2. Section Leaving H. Qtrs at 1.30 p and one hand cart & half. Limber and carrying party will be provided for No. 1. Section Leaving H. Qtrs at 1.45 p

6. Handcarts will go no further than the Railway Station, where they will unload under cover from view. Gun teams will leave Station at intervals of not less than 10 minutes.

7 Carrying Parties will help the 33 M.G.C. back. 2nd Lt Tiptaft will be held responsible that this is carried out.

8 All trench Stores to be taken over and copy sent to 62nd Hd Qtrs by 10pm 18th inst.

9. Telephone Installation will be in both Section H Qtrs

10. On completion of relief section will wire "Budget."

11 2nd Lt Boswell will hand over to 2nd Lt Brown two company notice boards from J. All bombs brought down to day will be taken up to morrow and counted as Stationary Trench Stores "in Lieu"

12. Orderly Officer to-morrow Lt Warren

10.5 p

17.8.16

C F Dingwall Capt and Adjt
62 Co M.G.C.

7.

Orders by Capt. G. G. N. Lodge
Commanding 62 Co. Machine Gun Corps

1. Orderly Officer tomorrow
2nd Lt Boswell.

Attention is recalled to the duties of Company Orderly Officer which will be found in Hd Qtrs.

2. Divine Service. Voluntary.

Soldiers Club. 7.30 am Holy Communion
9.30 pm Evening Service

3. Canteen.

A Company Canteen is opened at 11 Rue de la Taix. All profits will go to the benefit of the men of the company. To this end it is a kindness to the company to buy as much as possible there. There has been a card put up for suggestion. It is hoped that the present stock may be soon bought up to enable a new supply to be bought. Another Company Canteen will be opened in the Trenches on Monday.

19.8.16.

C. F. Dingwall Capt and Adjt
62 Machine Gun Company.

1

8

Orders by. Capt G. G. N. Lodge.
Commanding. 62 Co Royal. Machine Gun Corps.
In the field. 26.8.16. Tab I

1. Discipline

Before cleaning any part of a rifle the magazine will invariably be removed. and the bolt opened.

2 Identity. Discs.

It has been brought to notice that many men lately received into Field Ambulances and Casualty Clearing Station were not wearing an identity disc. Great difficulty has consequently been experienced in establishing the identity of those who were unconscious when admitted. Weekly inspection is to be made in all Units to ensure that the provisions of this paragraph are carried out.

3. Discipline

A practice appears to have arisen of one soldier only saluting when more than one are passing an Officer. This practice is to cease.

When several soldiers pass an Officer, unless they are being marched as a party, they will all salute, whether there are N.C.Os among them or not. All will take time from the man nearest to the officer.

When a party of men is being marched by a N.C.O or older soldier, the N.C.O. or man in charge of the party will give the order "Eyes right," or "Left" and himself salute.

When two or more men are standing or sitting about and an Officer passes them, the senior N.C.O. or oldest soldier will face the officer, call the rest to attention and alone salute.

Soldiers will salute in the manner laid down in the training manuals.

Officers must return the salutes of their subordinates with a definite motion of the hand and not perfunctorily, if more than one officer is present the senior alone will return the salute.

Officers will check lack of discipline in saluting and will report to the unit concerned the names of men who fail to salute them.
Officers commanding units will deal severely with men whose names are reported to them on this account.

4 Salutes.

The strictest attention of all Officers and Soldiers should be directed to studying the uniforms and rank distinction of our Allies and to the necessity of observing the obvious courtesies of saluting and returning salutes. Quite irrespective of rank, it should be an accepted rule that no officer or soldier passes or is passed by an Officer or soldier of the allied army without some act of recognition. When officers (Foreign) or soldiers salute British Officers all the officers so saluted will acknowledge the compliment, irrespective of who is senior.

5 Censorship. Postal. Restrictions

In conformity with regulations now in force throughout the British Empire; it is forbidden in future to despatch to enemy or neutral countries.

(1). Pictorial illustrations of any kind, This term includes picture postcards, cards with silk embroidered designs, illustrations cut from newspapers, magazines, or books.
(2) Newspapers, books, prospectuses, etc except when sent through the medium of publishers or authorised agents. Any articles or packets contravening this order found in the post by the Army Postal Service will be forwarded to the Censors at the Bases for disposal.

6 Steel. Helmets.

Officers and men in possession of steel helmets will invariably wear them when on duty, They are not to be carried attached to the pack. When on the Line of March.

7 Rubbish

In future units will ensure that all refuse is carefully examined before being taken to the incinerator for destruction.

All ranks are to be warned that on no account are they to loiter about in the vicinity of incinerators

8 Clothing.

Clean clothing can be issued to all N.C.O.s and men in the trenches at the commencement of next week. When this is issued all underclothing in whatever condition will be returned to Head Quarters.

9 All expended rounds of ammunition to be collected and sent down to H.d. Qtrs, every afternoon in Sand Bags. All R.E. indents for sections to be sent down with daily report orderly, this includes indent for ammunition.

10 Officers can always see G.R.O, 3rd Army R.O. Corps R.O Div R.O. and Brigade orders at Hd. Qtrs at any time of the day.

11 Divine Services will be issued later.

12 Orders for Royal Machine Gun emplacement, will be sent up this evening, they will be nailed on the back of the Co order board.

13 Section Officers and Transport Officer will render a return by 10. p.m. 27.8.16, the number of inoculated T.A.B. this information can be found at the back of pay book.

C. F. Dingwall. Capt & Adjutant
62 Co. R. Machine Gun Corps

Orders by Capt. G. G. N. Lodge.
Commanding 62. Co. R. M. G. C.
In the field. 26. 8. 16.

Part. II.

Reg. No.	Rank	Name.	Particulars of casualties etc., and Date.
Promotions and appointments.			
30907.	Act. Sgt.	Milthorp. F.	Promoted sergeant 14. 7. 16. to complete estb.
12564.	L. Cpl.	Tassell. W. C.	Granted pay of app. 7. 6. 16. vice. Roberts.
13282.	" "	May. T. A.	" " " " 4. 7. 16 vice. Meamns.
12559.	" "	Hope. G. B.	" " " " 15. 7. 16 " McWilliams
5041	Pte.	Sealy. T.	" " " 15. 7. 16 " Boag
5052.	"	Turner. W. C.	Appointed Lance Cpls unpaid. 24. 8. 16. Athy. G. O. C. 62. Ify. Bge.
6229	"	Foster. J.	
9672	"	Harris. E.	
9685	"	Reilly. S.	
31837.	"	Homes S.	

C. F. Dingwall Capt. and Adj.
62. Co. Royal. Machine Gun. Corps.

28. 8. 16

Orders by. Capt. G. G. N. Lodge.
Commanding 62. Co. Royal. Machine Gun Corps.
In the field.

I No 4. Section will relieve No 1. Sec. to morrow in I. right.

II Gun teams will start from Hd. Qtrs at 7.30 a.m. Hand carts will be provided for. Hand-carts not to go farther than station.

III Gun teams will take up their own belt boxes filled with ammunition. Nominal roll of gun teams can be seen at Hd. Qtrs.

IV. O.C. No. 4. Section will arrange for telephone orderly & runner.

V. O.C. No 1. Section will hand over to O.C. No. 4. all trench & company stores on separate lists which will be signed for, and a copy brought to Hd. Qtrs by 1.00 p.m.

VI Attention must be paid that each emplacement has a range card, and company notice board.

VII Trench Stores will also include indication board.

VIII. Teams will move off at 10 minutes intervals from Station. On completion of relief. O.C. No. 4. Section will wire "Goldflake."

IX. A circular memo has come round from "Lord Kitchener" memorial, to provide comforts for disabled Officers & Men. The C.O. hopes everybody will be able to provide something, not more than one Franc. Section commanders will collect subscription from each man & forward it to Hd. Qtrs not later than Wednesday 10. p.m. Subscription for Hd. Qtrs will be collected by Adjutant.

C. F. Dingwall Capt & Adjut.
62. Co R. M. G. C.

62nd Brigade.

21st Division.

62nd BRIGADE MACHINE GUN COMPANY

SEPTEMBER 1916.

Vol 7
62 MGC

Instructions regarding War Diaries and Intelligence Summaries are contained in F. S. Regs., Part II. and the Staff Manual respectively. Title pages will be prepared in manuscript.

Army Form C. 2118.

WAR DIARY
or
~~INTELLIGENCE SUMMARY.~~
(Erase heading not required.)

Place	Date 1916	Hour	Summary of Events and Information	Remarks and references to Appendices
ARRAS	Sept 1+2		In Trenches	
	3/4		Relieved during night by 104 Coy. R.M.G.C.	
	4	8.30pm	Marched to DAINVILLE. By motor lorry to GRANDE RULLECOURT, arriving about 1 a.m. 5/9/16. TRANSPORT BY ROAD.	
GRANDE RULLECOURT	5 to 11		Training + re-organization of Coy. proceeded with.	
	7		Route march. No. 1 section of this Coy. selected by Brig. Genl. RAWLINGS as smartest section or platoon in Brigade.	
	11		Transport left by road for ALBERT	
	12	4.30pm	Coy. left GRANDE RULLECOURT marched to REBREUVIETTE. Billeted for night.	
	13		Marched to FREVENT + entrained. Arrived ALBERT about 1 a.m. 14/9/16	
	14	1 a.m.	Marched to DERNANCOURT + bivouacked. TRANSPORT BY ROAD.	
DERNANCOURT	15		5 men each from 12th + 13th Northumberland Fus., 10th Yorks, + 1st Lincs. attached. 20 men in all.	
	16	8 a.m.	Marched via FRICOURT + MAMETZ to POMMIERS REDOUBT, + bivouacked.	
POMMIERS REDOUBT	17		Moved at dark from POMMIERS REDOUBT marched via MONTAUBAN.	Relieved

T2134. Wt. W708–776. 500000. 4/15. Sir J. C. & S.

Instructions regarding War Diaries and Intelligence Summaries are contained in F. S. Regs., Part II. and the Staff Manual respectively. Title Pages will be prepared in manuscript.

Army Form C. 2118.

WAR DIARY
or
INTELLIGENCE SUMMARY
(Erase heading not required.)

Place	Date	Hour	Summary of Events and Information	Remarks and references to Appendices
	Sept. (cont'd.) 17		Relieved 43rd Coy. R.M.G.C. in trenches before GUEUDECOURT. One section attached to each battalion in Brigade.	
GUEUDECOURT	18		CAPT LODGE ill. Lt DICKSON injured. 2Lt BROWN wounded. Command of Coy. taken over by Capt. C.F. DINGWALL	
do	20		One ~~section~~ gun team withdrawn into reserve	
	23		Relieved by 64th Coy. Marched to FRICOURT CAMP	
FRICOURT CAMP	24	10am	Arrived & bivouacked. Total casualties 1 man killed. 3 officers & 12 OR wounded 3 OR missing. Total 19. During night enemy aeroplane dropped bombs. No damage or casualties.	
	25	8am	Marched via MAMETZ & MONTAUBAN. Arrived at point near TRONES WOOD. 12.30pm & bivouacked.	
	26	night	Relieved 64th Coy. in trenches E of GUEUDECOURT. One section with each battalion as before.	
	27		Heavy bombardment for 40 mins. Some casualties.	
	29		Relieved by 61st Coy. Total casualties 2 OR killed 10 wounded. Total 12. Bivouacked near TRONES WOOD	
	30		Marched to BUIRE & billeted	

[illegible] [illegible]
C.F. Dingwall Capt

2449 Wt. W14957/M90 750,000 1/16 J.B.C. & A. Forms/C.2118/12.

Vol 8

Sheet I

Army Form C. 2118.

Instructions regarding War Diaries and Intelligence Summaries are contained in F. S. Regs., Part II. and the Staff Manual respectively. Title Pages will be prepared in manuscript.

WAR DIARY

or

~~INTELLIGENCE SUMMARY~~

(Erase heading not required.)

62 Company R.M.G.C.

Place	Date	Hour	Summary of Events and Information	Remarks and references to Appendices
NEAR TRONES WOOD.	Oct. 1.	9.30	Marched to BUIRE and billeted.	
BUIRE.	2.	11.30	Transport moved by road to MOUFLERS.	
	3.	2.0	Company entrained at EDGE HILL for LONGPRES.	
LONGPRES	4.	4 a.m.	Marched from LONGPRES to MOUFLERS and billeted.	
MOUFLEURS.	6.		15 O.R. joined for duty and were taken on strength of company.	
"	7.	7.30.	Marched to LONGPRES with transport and entrained for JOCQUERIELS.	
	8.	4 a.m.	Arrived JOCQUEREILS. marched to LAPUGNOY.	
LAPUGNOY	9.	1.30	Marched to NOEUX-LE-MINES.	
NOEUX-LE-MINES.	10.	1.	Marched to VERMELLES and relieved 24 COMPANY R.M.G.C. 12 guns in the line 4 guns in Reserve.	
VERMELLES	11.		CAPT. H. E. WATKINS and 1 O.R. arrived from 103 COMPANY. RMGC.	
	12.		CAPT. H. E. WATKINS assumed command of the Company.	
"	18		No 3 Section relieved No 1 Section, No 1 Section relieved No 4 Section. Indirect Fire was employed during this period.	
"	19.		2/LT. G. LESLIE, 6th BATT. SEAFORTHS. joined for duty.	
"	24		CAPT. C. F. DINGWALL & 1 O.R. proceeded to join 90 COMPANY R. M. G. C.	

2449 Wt. W14957/M90 750,000 1/16 J.B.C. & A. Forms/C.2118/12.

Instructions regarding War Diaries and Intelligence Summaries are contained in F. S. Regs., Part II. and the Staff Manual respectively. Title Pages will be prepared in manuscript.

WAR DIARY
or
~~INTELLIGENCE SUMMARY~~

(Erase heading not required.)

Sheet II

Army Form C. 2118.

62 Company R.M.G.C.

Place	Date	Hour	Summary of Events and Information	Remarks and references to Appendices
VERMELLES	Oct 26.		No 4 Section relieved No 3 Section. No 3 Section relieved No 1 Section. Half No 2 Section relieved the ~~other~~ half No 2 Section. Indirect fire was employed during this period, Day + night. Ends. H. S. Watkins. Capt.	

2449 Wt. W14957/M90 750,000 1/16 J.B.C. & A. Forms/C.2118/12.

Sheet I

62 Company

Machine Gun Corps.

Vol 9

21

Army Form C. 2118.

Instructions regarding War Diaries and Intelligence Summaries are contained in F. S. Regs., Part II. and the Staff Manual respectively. Title Pages will be prepared in manuscript.

WAR DIARY
or
~~INTELLIGENCE SUMMARY~~

(Erase heading not required.)

Place	Date	Hour	Summary of Events and Information	Remarks and references to Appendices
VERMELLES.	3/11/16	7.30a.m.	No 1. Section relieved No 4 Section in the VILLAGE LINE. No 4 Section relieved No 3 Section in RESERVE LINE. Indirect fire was employed day and night on Selected Targets. Reserve Section at H.Q in VERMELLES were employed during daytime in repairing CHAPEL ALLEY. 12 Guns in Trenches 4 guns in reserve.	
VERMELLES	4/11/16		8 O.R. (attached) returned to their units.	
"	7/11/16		2/LIEUT. W.P. DEAN reported for duty and was taken on strength of Company	
VERMELLES.	10/11/16	7.30a.m.	No 3 Section relieved No 1 Section in VILLAGE LINE. No 1 Section relieved No 4 Section in RESERVE LINE. 2 GUNS No 2 Section relieved the other 2 GUNS No 2 Section in HIGHLAND TRENCH. Indirect fire was employed day and night on Selected Targets.	
"	11/11/16		10 O.R. reported for duty (to complete new Establishment) and were taken on strength of Company.	
"	18/11/16.		GUN from V.36 VILLAGE LINE moved to new Emplacement in DEVON LANE.	
"	19/11/16		No 4 Section relieved No 3 Section in VILLAGE LINE. No 3 Section relieved No 4 Section in RESERVE LINE. Indirect fire was employed day and night on Selected Targets.	

2449 Wt. W14957/M90 750,000 1/16 J.B.C. & A. Forms/C.2118/12.

Instructions regarding War Diaries and Intelligence Summaries are contained in F. S. Regs., Part II. and the Staff Manual respectively. Title Pages will be prepared in manuscript.

Sheet II

Army Form C. 2118.

WAR DIARY
or
~~INTELLIGENCE SUMMARY~~
(Erase heading not required.)

62 Company
Machine Gun Corps

Place	Date	Hour	Summary of Events and Information	Remarks and references to Appendices
VERMELLES	20/11/16.		Left gun in HIGHLAND TRENCH moved to vicinity of HAIRPIN CRATERS.	
"	27/11/16.		2/LIEUT. D. YATES and 2 O.Rs proceeded to CAMIERS to attend a course at the MACHINE GUN SCHOOL.	
"	27/11/16.		No 1 Section relieved No 4 Section in VILLAGE LINE. No 4 Section relieved No 3 Section in RESERVE LINE. Indirect fire was employed day and night on selected Targets.	

Ends:

[illegible] 2/Lt.
Commanding 62 Coy. M.G.C.

2449 Wt. W14957/M90 750,000 1/16 J.B.C. & A. Forms/C.2118/12.

Instructions regarding War Diaries and Intelligence Summaries are contained in F. S. Regs., Part II. and the Staff Manual respectively. Title pages will be prepared in manuscript.

WAR DIARY
or
INTELLIGENCE SUMMARY.
(Erase heading not required.)

SHEET I

Army Form C. 2118.

62 Company Machine Gun Corps.

Vol 10

Place	Date	Hour	Summary of Events and Information	Remarks and references to Appendices
VERMELLES.	5/12/16	7.a.m.	Section relief. No 3 Section relieved No 1 Section in VILLAGELINE. No 1 Section relieved No 4 Section in RESERVE LINE.	
"	30/11/16 to 5/12/16		Indirect fire was employed on selected targets behind the enemies line, day and night. 12 guns in Trenches 4 guns in Reserve at VERMELLES.	
VERMELLES	11/12/16	7a.m.	Section relief No 1 Section relieved No 2 Section in RESERVELINE (RIGHT) No 3 Section relieved No 4 Section in RESERVELINE (LEFT) No 4 Section relieved No 3 Section in VILLAGELINE.	
	5/12/16 to 11/12/16		Indirect fire was employed, night and day, on selected Targets behind enemies line. 12 guns in Trenches 4 guns in Reserve at VERMELLES.	
VERMELLES	12/12/16		4 O.R's reported for duty and were taken on strength of Company.	
"	12/12/16		3 O.R's proceeded to Divisional School for a course in Signalling.	
"	14/12/16		4 O.R's reported for duty and were taken on Strength of Company.	
VERMELLES	17/12/16	7a.m.	Section Relief. No 2 Section relieved No 4 Section VILLAGELINE, No 4 Section relieved No 3 Section RESERVELINE (RIGHT). No 3 Section relieved No 1 Section RESERVELINE (LEFT). Extra guns sent up to Emplacement S2. DEVON LANE. 13 guns in Trenches 3 guns in Reserve at VERMELLES.	

T2134. Wt. W708–776. 500000. 4/15. Sir J. C. & S.

Instructions regarding War Diaries and Intelligence Summaries are contained in F. S. Regs., Part II. and the Staff Manual respectively. Title pages will be prepared in manuscript.

WAR DIARY
or
INTELLIGENCE SUMMARY.
(Erase heading not required.)

SHEET 2

62 Company Machine Gun Corps.

Army Form C. 2118.

Place	Date	Hour	Summary of Events and Information	Remarks and references to Appendices
VERMELLES	12/12/16 to 17/12/16		Indirect fire was employed, day and night, on selected targets behind the enemies line.	
"	17/12/16		LIEUT. A. BIAGOTT reported for duty and was taken on strength of Company.	
"	17/12/16		32 O.R.S transferred to M.G.C. from 62nd Infantry Brigade.	
"	20/12/16		Capt. H.E. WATKINS admitted to Field Ambulance. LIEUT. J. DODSON took over command of Company. Extra guns sent to K DUMP. (14 guns in Trenches).	
"	23/12/16		Heavy bombardment of our Trenches by enemy, 6 Casualties 4 killed 2 wounded.	
"	26/12/16	2 pm	Company relieved by 71 Machine Gun Company 14 guns in Trenches 2 guns in Reserve at VERMELLES. After relief 62 Company marched to billets at HOUCHIN.	
HOUCHIN	27/12/16	9:30 am	Marched to billets at MARLES-LES-MINES.	
MARLES-LES-MINES	27/12/16 to 30/12/16		Billeted at MARLES-LES-MINES. Guns, gun equipment, and service equipment thoroughly overhauled. Training of Company carried on.	
MARLES-LES-MINES	31/12/16	10 am	Marched to billets at REVEILLON.	

Ends

J. Dodson Lt
Commanding 62 Coy. M.G.C.

T2134. Wt. W708-776. 500000. 4/15. Sir J. C. & S.

Instructions regarding War Diaries and Intelligence Summaries are contained in F. S. Regs., Part II. and the Staff Manual respectively. Title pages will be prepared in manuscript.

WAR DIARY
or
~~INTELLIGENCE SUMMARY.~~
(Erase heading not required.)

62 Company Machine Gun Corps
Sheet I

Army Form C. 2118.

Vol XI

Place	Date	Hour	Summary of Events and Information	Remarks and references to Appendices
REVILLION	1/1/17 to 27/1/17		Company in Rest billets at REVILLION. a systematic training of the whole company was carried out during this period.	
"	19/1/17	9 a.m.	Company was inspected by Brig Gen C. G. RAWLING Commanding 62 INFANTRY BRIGADE.	
	15/1/17		L/Cpl No 71837 J. TAYLOR proceeded to CAMIERS for a course of instruction at the MACHINE GUN SCHOOL.	
"	2/1/17		10 O.R's joined from Base and were taken on strength of Company.	
	3/1/17		4 O.R's joined from Base and were taken on strength of Company.	
"	24/1/17		1 NCO + 1 O.R. proceeded to Base for evacuation to United Kingdom to take up Duties at the M.G.T.C. GRANTHAM.	
"	25/1/17	8.30 a.m.	5 Officers proceeded to Trenches in front of PHILOSOPHE to reconnoitre the line.	
"	27/1/17	9 a.m.	Company entrained at CHOCQUES and proceeded to POPERINGHE	
POPERINGHE			and marched into huts at H Camp Near VOX VRIE FARM.	
VOX VRIE FARM	29/1/17	11 a.m.	Six Officers proceeded to St. SIXTE to reconnoitre the strong points	

T2134. Wt. W708-776. 500000. 4/15. Sir J. C. & S.

Instructions regarding War Diaries and Intelligence Summaries are contained in F. S. Regs., Part II. and the Staff Manual respectively. Title pages will be prepared in manuscript.

WAR DIARY
or
INTELLIGENCE SUMMARY.
(Erase heading not required.)

Sheet II.

Army Form C. 2118.

Place	Date	Hour	Summary of Events and Information	Remarks and references to Appendices
VOX VRIE FARM	29/1/17		behind the LINE occupied by THE BELGIAN ARMY.	
"	29/1/17	11am	No 4 Section attached to 12th BATT. NORTHUMBERLAND FUSILIERS	
			No 1 Section attached to 10th BATT. YORKS REGT.	
"	29/1/17 to 31/1/17		No 2 and 3 sections carried on training while waiting for orders to proceed to advanced B.H.Q at St SIXTE.	

Ends.

H. G. Watkins. Capt.
Comdg 62 Coy. M. G. Corps

T2134. Wt. W708-776. 500000. 4/15. Sir J. C. & S.

62nd Coy M G Corps

Instructions regarding War Diaries and Intelligence Summaries are contained in F. S. Regs., Part II. and the Staff Manual respectively. Title pages will be prepared in manuscript.

WAR DIARY
or
~~INTELLIGENCE SUMMARY.~~
(Erase heading not required.)

62 Company
Machine Gun Corps
Sheet I

Army Form C. 2118.

Vol 17

Place	Date	Hour	Summary of Events and Information	Remarks and references to Appendices
VOX VRIE			Company in Huts. No 2 & 3 sections at H. Camp.	
FARM.	1-2-17		No 1 section attached to 10th BATT YORKS REGT	
"	to		No 4 section attached to 12th BATT NORTHUMBERLAND FUSILERS,	
"	14-2-17		carried on systematic training during this period.	
"	15-2-17	1-40pm.	Company entrained at HOPOUTRE and proceeded to CHOCQUES and	
			marched to Billets at BETHUNE.	
BETHUNE	16-2-17	9am	Company proceeded to trenches QUARRES SECTOR and relieved the	
VERMELLES	"	11-am	71st Company. M. G. C. No. 1. section to VILLAGE LINE. No 2 section RIGHT	
VERMELLES	"	"	SECTOR, No 4 section LEFT SECTOR, No 3 section in reserve at VERMELLES	
"			with Company H. Q. 12 guns in line, 4 guns in reserve.	
"	17-2-17		Indirect fire was carried out day and night on selected targets	
"			behind the enemies lines, and spare men worked all night on gun	
"			emplacements which were falling in owing to thaw.	
"	20-2-17	11am	3 sections relieved by 2nd MACHINE GUN SQUADRON and proceeded to LA BOURSE	
"			in billets. No 1 section remaining at VERMELLES attached to 2nd M.G	
"			SQUADRON.	

T2134. Wt. W708–776. 500000. 4/15. Sir J. C. & S.

Instructions regarding War Diaries and Intelligence Summaries are contained in F. S. Regs., Part II. and the Staff Manual respectively. Title pages will be prepared in manuscript.

WAR DIARY
or
~~INTELLIGENCE SUMMARY.~~
(Erase heading not required.)

62 Company
Machine Gun Corps
Sheet 2.

Army Form C. 2118.

Place	Date	Hour	Summary of Events and Information	Remarks and references to Appendices
LA BOURSE	21-2-17	9am	General clean up of Company.	
"	22-2-17	8-30am	2 OFFICERS and 60 O.R. supplied daily by Company for working party to	
"	25-2-17		clear trenches in QUARRIES SECTOR.	
"	28-2-17	10-am	Company minus No 1 section proceeded to BETHUNE to take up	
"	"		billets. No 1 section after being relieved by 71st M. G. Coy will join	
"	"		the company at BETHUNE	
VOX VRIE. Farm	5-2-17		Lt DODSON evacuated to Base	
"	13-2-17		1 O.R sent to M. G. Training ~~[illegible]~~ Centre Grantham.	
VERMELLES	17-2-17		1 O.R. joined from Base.	
LA. BOURSE	26-2-17		Lt TIPTAFT & 2 O.R. proceeded to M. G. School	
			Ends	
			H.S. Watkins, Capt. Commanding 62 Coy. M. G. C.	

T2134. Wt. W708-776. 500000. 4/15. Sir J. C. & S.

...uctions regarding War Diaries and Intelligence ~~Summaries~~ are contained in F. S. Regs., Part II. and the Staff Manual respectively. Title pages will be prepared in manuscript.

WAR DIARY
or
~~INTELLIGENCE SUMMARY.~~
(Erase heading not required.)

12nd Company
Machine Gun Corps

Army Form C. 2118.

Sheet 1 Vol 13

Place	Date	Hour	Summary of Events and Information	Remarks and references to Appendices
LABOURSE	25.2.17		Marched from LABOURSE to BETHUNE.	
BETHUNE	1.3.17		Marched from BETHUNE to ROBECQ.	
ROBECQ	2.3.17		Marched from ROBECQ to LA MIQUELLERIE	
LA MIQUELLERIE	3.3.17 to		Systematic	
"	8.3.17		Training	
"	6.3.17		Capt: N.E. PARROTT took over command of Company	
"	"		Capt. H.E. WATKINS admitted to Field Ambulance	
"	"		2/Lt: H.V.J HILL left for ENGLAND to join INDIAN Army	
	9.3.17		Marched from LA MIQUELLERIE to LIGNY-LEZ-AIRE	
Ligny-lez-AIRE	10.3.17		" " LIGNY-lez-AIRE to BETHONVAL.	
BETHONVAL	11.3.17		" " BETHONVAL to SERICOURT.	
SERICOURT	12.3.17		" " SERICOURT to HALLOY.	
HALLOY	13.3.17 to		Systematic	
"	24.3.17		Training	
"	14.3.17		2 O.R. joined from Base Depot.	
	18.3.17		Lt. J BOSWELL proceeded to LATTRE St QUENTIN on course – Recognition of Aircraft	

T2134. Wt. W708—776. 500000. 4/15. Sir J. C. & S.

Instructions regarding War Diaries and Intelligence Summaries are contained in F. S. Regs., Part II. and the Staff Manual respectively. Title pages will be prepared in manuscript.

WAR DIARY
or
INTELLIGENCE SUMMARY.
(Erase heading not required.)

[illegible] Company Machine Gun Corps
Sheet 2

Army Form C. 2118.

Place	Date	Hour	Summary of Events and Information	Remarks and references to Appendices
HALLOY	18·3·17		Lt. W. R. TIPTAFT rejoined from M. G. School. Lt. MILWARD joined from Base Depot	
"	23·3·17		2 O.R evacuated	
"	24·3·17		Capt. W. B. HORSBURGH assumes command.	
	25·3·17		Marched to BIENVILLIERS-AU-BOIS.	
BIENVILLIERS AU BOIS	26·3·17		" " HAMELINCOURT to relieve 198th M. G. Company.	
	27·3·17		Relief completed in early morning. No 4 Section in right sector	
	"		No 3 Section in reserve at HAMELINCOURT. No 1 Section in left sector	
	"		No 2 Section in Reserve at BOISLEUX-AU-MONT. Company H.Q established at HAMELINCOURT.	
HAMELINCOURT.	31·3·17	2 am.	No 2 Section moves up from BOISLEUX-AU-MONT to the right of No 4 Section and is attached to 1st LINCOLN'S. No 3 remaining at Company H.Q. in Reserve.	
HAMELINCOURT	29·3·17	3 pm.	Lieut MILWARD. H. H admitted to F. A.	

Ends

W. B. Horsburgh Capt Commdg
62 Company. M. G. C.

T2134. Wt. W708-776. 500000. 4/15. Sir J. C. & S.

Instructions regarding War Diaries and Intelligence Summaries are contained in F. S. Regs., Part II. and the Staff Manual respectively. Title pages will be prepared in manuscript.

WAR DIARY
or
~~INTELLIGENCE~~ SUMMARY.
(Erase heading not required.)

62 Company M. G. C.

Army Form C. 2118.

SHEET. I. 62nd Coy M G Corps

Vol 14

Place	Date	Hour	Summary of Events and Information	Remarks and references to Appendices
CROISILLES	1-4-17		LT MILLWARD H. H. evacuated to Base.	
"	2-4-17		Company took part in an advance on the CROISILLES – HENIN sur	
"	"		COJEUL Rd. which was captured after a little fighting from T. 17. b. 6. 1. and	
"	"		T. 3. b. 1. 9. SHEET 51B S.W. 1/20,000. No I Section advanced with ~~with~~	
"	"		the 12th NORTHUMBERLAND FUSILIERS on the left front from T. 9. b. 7. 3	
"	"		to T. 3. a. 3. 4. No 4 Section with 1st LINCOLNS' Regt from T. 16. b. 2. 8. to	
"	"		T. 9. b. 7. 5. No 3 Section with 13th NORTHUMBERLAND FUSILIERS from T. 17. c. 7. 6	
"	"		to T. 16. b. 2. 8. No 2 Section remaining in reserve at HAMELINCOURT.	
"	"		Casualties. 4 O.R. killed. 3 O.R. wounded.	
"	"		Capt Parrott. J rejoined 110th M. G. Company.	
HAMELINCOURT	4-4-17		Relieved by 110th M. G. Company and billetted at HAMELINCOURT.	
HENDECOURT	5-4-17		Company marched to HENDECOURT in Divisional Reserve.	
"	7-4-17		LT DEAN. W & 2/Lt Leslie. G. admitted F Ambulance. 2/Lt. Walter joined from Base	
"	8-4-17		Company marched from HENDECOURT to BOIRY ST MARTIN. Nucleus party	
			2 officers & 21. O.R marched to ADINFER and are attached to No 2 Train	
			A.S.C	

T2134. Wt. W708–776. 500000. 4/15. Sir J. C. & S.

Instructions regarding War Diaries and Intelligence Summaries are contained in F. S. Regs., Part II. and the Staff Manual respectively. Title pages will be prepared in manuscript.

WAR DIARY
or
INTELLIGENCE SUMMARY.
(*Erase heading not required.*)

62 Company M. G. C.

SHEET 2

Army Form C. 2118.

Place	Date	Hour	Summary of Events and Information	Remarks and references to Appendices
BOIRY ST				
MARTIN	9-4-17		1. O.R. wounded	
"	10-4-17		No I Section assisted the advance of the 89th Brigade with a barrage	
"			fired from T.2 d at Hindenburgh line at N.27. b. & D. & N 28 a. & C. rounds	
"			fired 50,000. No 3 Section in reserve to 64th Brigade guarding railway	
"			line S 22. & S 28. Lt Colley J admitted F.A.	
"	11-4-17		Company relieved 64th M. G. Coy in the line. No 2 Section in approximately	
"			T5.a.5.3 to T 4. b. 9. 7 and came under the orders of the 1st LINCOLNS Regt.	
"			No 4 Section on N.34 & T.4. and came under the command of O.C 13. Northumberland	
"			Fusiliers. No 3 Section in support in the Sunken Rd N. 34. c & T.4.a. No 1 Section	
"			in reserve (Brigade) in Sunken Rd T. 9. b.	
BOYELLES	12-4-17		LIEUT Spry. W. wounded. Company H. Qrs advanced BOYELLES.	
"	13-4-17		1 O.R. wounded.	
"	14-4-17		Company relieved by 19th M. G. Coy and bivouaced in BOYELLES for the night	
"	15-4-17		Nucleus party rejoined from ADINFER. Company moved to BRETENCOURT	
BRETENCOURT	16-4-17		4 O.R reinforcements joined	
	18-4-17		Lt DODSON rejoined from Base	

T2134. Wt. W708-776. 500000. 4/15. Sir J. C. & S.

Instructions regarding War Diaries and Intelligence Summaries are contained in F. S. Regs., Part II. and the Staff Manual respectively. Title pages will be prepared in manuscript.

WAR DIARY or ~~INTELLIGENCE SUMMARY.~~

(*Erase heading not required.*)

62 Company M G C

SHEET 3

Army Form C. 2118.

Place	Date	Hour	Summary of Events and Information	Remarks and references to Appendices
BRETENCOURT	20-4-17		5 O.R. joined from Base	
"	22-4-17		No 1 & 2 Sections marched to ACHVILLE & DAINVILLE for anti air craft work, guarding ammunition dumps. 2/Lt TILLOTSON. H. joined from Base	
"	24417		Company moved to MERCATEL	
MERCATEL	26-4-17		Company moved to BOYELLES and remained in Divisional Reserve	
BOYELLES	27-4-17		2 O.R. joined from Base	
"	28-4-17		LIEUT. A. BIAGOTT proceeded to MACHINEGUN SCHOOL for advanced Course.	
	29-4-17		2/LIEUT WALTER evacuated to C.C.S.	
"	29-4-17		Company less No4 SECTION marched to T 20 b. and relieved No110 Company. No1 Section took over positions (a) T17a. 7.5. (b) T11d 7.6. (c) T11d 7.9. (d) T5d 8.1. and came under the orders of G.C. 1st LINCOLN. REGT. No2 Section took over positions (a) T24 b 4.7 (b) T18.c 55 15. (c) T17c 70.25. (d) T11d 8.1. and came under the orders of G.C. 10th YORKS REGT. No 3 Section remained in Reserve at Company Headquarters at T 20 b. Relief was completed by 11.30 p.m. No4 Section under the orders of G.C. 13th NORTHUMBERLAND FUSILIERS relieved one Section of No 64 Company and took over positions (a) T11d 95 90 (b) T5d 00.40. Two guns remained in reserve at Section Headquarters near T4d 90.10.	

T2134. Wt. W708–776. 50000. 4/15. Sir J. C. & S.

Instructions regarding War Diaries and Intelligence Summaries are contained in F. S. Regs., Part II. and the Staff Manual respectively. Title pages will be prepared in manuscript.

WAR DIARY

or

~~INTELLIGENCE SUMMARY.~~

(Erase heading not required.)

62 Company
M G C.
Sheet 4.

Army Form C. 2118.

Place	Date	Hour	Summary of Events and Information	Remarks and references to Appendices
	30/4/17	3.30am	Gun at T 17 a 7 5 fired on Target U 7 a 0.8 rounds fired 500, as requested by C.O 1st LINCOLN REGT.	
		12.40am	Gun at T 24 b 4 7 fired at Target U 7 c 9.9 to U 7 d 2 0. Rounds fired 2,000.	
			Gun at T 18 c 55 15 fired at Target U 13 b 2.9 to U 14 a 1.1 Rounds fired 2.500.	
	30/4/17		No 15632 L/Cpl J. A. WRIGHT awarded Bar to MILITARY MEDAL. No 35181 Pte B DUCKHAM. awarded MILITARY MEDAL.	
			ENDS.	
			W.B. Horsburgh Capt OC. 62 M.G. Coy	

T2134. Wt. W708–776. 500000. 4/15. Sir J. C. & S.

Instructions regarding War Diaries and Intelligence Summaries are contained in F. S. Regs., Part II. and the Staff Manual respectively. Title pages will be prepared in manuscript.

WAR DIARY

or

~~INTELLIGENCE SUMMARY.~~

(Erase heading not required.)

62nd Coy. M.G. Corps

~~62 COMPANY~~

MACHINE GUN CORPS.

Sheet I

Army Form C. 2118.

Vol 15

Place	Date	Hour	Summary of Events and Information	Remarks and references to Appendices
NE ST. LEGER	1/5/17.		2/Lt. C. J. COLLEY rejoined for duty from Field Ambulance.	
			Company in Trenches in front of FONTAINE-LE-CROISILLES. Gun at T17a. 7.5	
		9.0 to 9.45 p.m. 6.30 a.m.	fired at U7a 4.9 to U7a 9.0. Rounds fired 2.000.	
		1.45 a.m. to 4.30 a.m.	Gun at T18c 6.1. fired at Target U7c 9.9. to U7d 2.1. Rounds fired 1.500.	
		1.45 a.m. to 4.30 a.m.	Gun at T24b 40.75 fired at Target U13b 2.9. to U14c 1.9. Rounds fired 2.000.	
			This Gun position was heavily shelled about 4 a.m. 1 O.R. Wounded.	
	2/5/17.		No 8. Sub-Section under 2/Lt. H. TILLOTSON attached to No 1 Section and comes	
			under Orders of O.C. 1st LINCOLN REGT.	
		1.35 a.m. to 2 a.m.	Gun at T18c 6.1 fired at Target U7c 9.9. to U7d 2.1. Rounds fired 2.000.	
		1 a.m. to 3 a.m.	Gun at T24b 40.75 fired at Target U13b 2.9. to U14c 1.9. Rounds fired 2.000.	
		9.45 to 3 a.m.	Gun at T17a 7.5. fired at Target U7a 4.9 to U7a 9.0. Rounds fired 2.500.	
			Company Headquarters moved to T21d 7.8.	
	3/5/17.		Machine Gun Barrage given to assist Infantry during attack on FONTAINE-LE-CROISILLES and FONTAINE WOOD. Zero at 3.45 a.m.	
		3.45 to 4 a.m.	Gun at T11d 90.20. enfiladed road at U1d 50.70 to U2a 00.15. Rounds fired 2.570.	
		3.45 to 5.40 a.m.	Gun at T17b 70.20 enfiladed sunken road from U8a 20.70 to U7b 80.40. Rounds fired 9.000.	

Instructions regarding War Diaries and Intelligence Summaries are contained in F. S. Regs., Part II. and the Staff Manual respectively. Title pages will be prepared in manuscript.

WAR DIARY
or
~~INTELLIGENCE SUMMARY.~~
(Erase heading not required.)

62 COMPANY.
MACHINE GUN CORPS.
Sheet II

Army Form C. 2118.

Place	Date	Hour	Summary of Events and Information	Remarks and references to Appendices
	3/5/17	3.45 a.m. to 6.40 a.m.	Gun at T 18 c 60.20 traversed from U 14 a 25.50 to U 14 c 50.80. Rounds fired 12.500.	
		3.45 a.m. to 6.15 a.m.	Gun at T 24 b 45.80 enfiladed Trench from U 7 d 90.95 to U 8 a 50.50. Rounds fired 10.500.	
		3.45 a.m. to 6.15 a.m.	Gun at T 5 d 70.80 traversed Sunken Road from U 8 a to U 8 c. Rounds fired 11.000.	
		3.45 a.m. to 6.40 a.m.	Gun at T 17 a. 60.60. traversed area from U 8 c 30.30 to U 14 a. 50.30. Rounds fired 13,000	
			Gun position at T 11 d 90.20 was heavily shelled. ~~position~~ Gun moved to new position at T 11 d 80.60. No 7. Sub-Section under LT. W.R. TIPTAFT. under Orders of G.C. 13th NORTHUMBERLAND FUSILIERS. took up positions O.31 c 1.5 and N.36 d. 6.2.	
			1. O.R. Wounded.	
	4/5/17	9.5 a.m.	LT. D. YATES. wounded. Company Headquarters moved to T 5. b. 8.8. in HINDENBURG SUPPORT LINE. Following relief took place. No 1 Section in Reserve at Company Headquarters at T 5 b. 8.8. under Orders of G.C. 12th NORTHUMBERLAND FUSILIERS. No 3 Sub-Section moved to positions T 6 b 3.3. and T 6 b 6.5. and came under Orders of G.C. 12th NORTH. Fus. No 6. Sub. Section moved to positions O 31 c. 5.5. and O 31 c. 7.9. and came under Orders of G.C. 13th NORTH. FUS. No 7 Sub-Section remained in positions O. 31 c. 1.5. and N 36 d 6.2. No 8 Sub. Section took up positions at N. 35 a. 1.0 and N 35 a. 4.3. and came under the Orders of G.C. 1st LINCOLN. REGT.	

T2134. Wt. W708–776. 500000. 4/15. Sir J. C. & S.

Instructions regarding War Diaries and Intelligence Summaries are contained in F. S. Regs., Part II. and the Staff Manual respectively. Title pages will be prepared in manuscript.

WAR DIARY
or
~~INTELLIGENCE SUMMARY.~~
(Erase heading not required.)

62 COMPANY
MACHINE GUN CORPS.
Sheet III

Army Form C. 2118.

Place	Date	Hour	Summary of Events and Information	Remarks and references to Appendices
	4/5/17		No 2 Section remained in its present position under orders of G.C. 10th YORKS. REGT.	
Nr HENIN.	"	5.30pm	Transport moved to T2c. 8.4.	
			12 guns of 64 COMPANY attached to 62 INFANTRY BRIGADE.	
	6/5/17.		1. O.R. Wounded.	
	7/5/17		LT. W. P. DEAN. returned to duty from M G C BASE DEPOT.	
	8/5/17.		4 guns of 62 COMPANY and 3 guns of 64 COMPANY in Brown Trench from T6a. 5. 6 to N36d 9.6. fired during night at FONTAINE WOOD.	
			1 gun of 64 COMPANY at T6a.4.4. fired during night at FONTAINE. WOOD.	
			2 guns of 64 COMPANY in PUG LANE TRENCH near T6b. fired during the night at FONTAINE WOOD. Rounds fired during the night 30.000.	
			No 2 Section under orders of G.C. 10th YORKS. REGT attached to 110 INFANTRY BRIGADE.	
	9/5/17.		No 2 Section attached to 110 INF. BDE. was relieved by 1 Section of 110 COMPANY. After relief No 2 Section went into bivouacs at T20b.	
			4 guns of 62 Company and 3 guns of 64 Company in Brown Trench and 1 gun of 64 COMPANY at T6a 4.4. fired at FONTAINE WOOD during the night. Rounds fired 24.000.	
	10/5/17.		53. INF. BDE. took over all positions NORTH of HINDENBURG SUPPORT. LINE.	

Instructions regarding War Diaries and Intelligence Summaries are contained in F. S. Regs., Part II. and the Staff Manual respectively. Title pages will be prepared in manuscript.

WAR DIARY
or
~~INTELLIGENCE~~ SUMMARY.
(Erase heading not required.)

62 COMPANY.
MACHINE GUN CORPS.
Sheet 4.

Army Form C. 2118.

Place	Date	Hour	Summary of Events and Information	Remarks and references to Appendices
Nr HENIN.	10/5/17	–	No 1 and 4 Sections relieved by 2 Sections of 53 COMPANY. after relief No 1 & 2 Sections went into bivouacs at T2 c. 8.4. COMPANY HEADQUARTERS moved to T2 c 8.4.	
	11/5/17	–	No 3 Section and 1 Section of 64 COMPANY attached to 62 INF BDE. were relieved by 2 Sections of 98 COMPANY. after relief No 3 Section went into bivouacs at T2 c 8.4.	
	12/5/17	5.30 a.m.	COMPANY less No 2 Section marched to rest billets at BLAIRVILLE. COMPANY Headquarters in the QUARRY.	
BLAIRVILLE.		12.	No 2 Section rejoined Company.	
"	13/5/17	2 p.m.	No 5 Sub-Section under 2/LT. H. TILLOTSON proceeded to MERCATEL to guard DUMPS against Hostile Aircraft. Gun positions M29c 70.70. and M 29 d 85.05.	
	14/5/17		2/LT. G. LESLIE rejoined from M.G.C. Base Depot. 4 O.R. reported from Base and were taken on ~~strength~~ of Company.	
	19/5/17	10.45 a.m.	COMPANY was inspected by G.O.C. 21st DIVISION. Transport was inspected by G.C. 21st DIVISIONAL TRAIN. The G.O.C. presented MILITARY MEDAL RIBAND to No. 15237 Sgt. W. ARNOTT. No 15632 Corp. J. A. WRIGHT. (BAR). No 35181. Pte. B. DUCKHAM.	
MERCATEL		9.5 a.m.	German aeroplane sighted passing over MERCATEL, at an altitude of 500 feet, proceeding in a WESTerly direction. Gun at M29c. 70.70 fired 69 rounds at it	

T2134. Wt. W708–776. 500000. 4/15. Sir J. C. & S.

Instructions regarding War Diaries and Intelligence Summaries are contained in F. S. Regs., Part II. and the Staff Manual respectively. Title pages will be prepared in manuscript.

WAR DIARY
or
~~INTELLIGENCE SUMMARY.~~
(Erase heading not required.)

62 COMPANY
MACHINE GUN CORPS.
Sheet 5.

Army Form C. 2118.

Place	Date	Hour	Summary of Events and Information	Remarks and references to Appendices
BLAIRVILLE	19/5/17		LT. A. BIAGOTT and 2 O.Rs rejoined from MACHINE GUN SCHOOL. CAMIERS.	
"		2 p.m.	A Revolver Shooting Competition was held at COMPANY. HEADQUARTERS.	
			1). Grouping competition (individuals). 1. No 84057 Pte. W.N. DOVE. $4\frac{7}{8}$ inch. group.	
			(2) No 42122 L/Cpl. H. HULME. $5\frac{5}{8}$ inch group. (3) No 42751 Pte. E. R. KETCHEL.	
			2). Application (Team of 4 men from each Section).	
			1) No 2 Section 86. (2) No 4 Section 76 (3) No 3 Section 73 (4) Transport 62 (5) No 1 Section 53.	
"	20/5/17	—	1 O.R. proceeded to MACHINE GUN SCHOOL CAMIERS. for Course of Instruction.	
"	20/5	2 p.m.	Company athletic sports were held in the Transport Field.	
	21/5/17		No 6 Sub-Section under 2/Lt. G. LESLIE proceeded to MERCATEL and relieved No 5 Sub. Section.	
	22/5/17		2 O.Rs reported for duty and were taken on strength of Company.	
		8 p.m.	No 6 Sub-Section at MERCATEL relieved by 4 LEWIS GUNS of the ROYAL SUSSEX REGT. (PIONEERS) 18th DIVISION. LT. W. R. TIPTAFT. and 2 O.Rs proceeded on leave to U. K.	
	23/5/17	2.30.	TACTICAL EXERCISE held near BERLES-AU-BOIS by VII CORPS. M.G.O.	
		5.30.	Lecture given by Lt.-Col. STEVENSON. 13th NORTHd. FUS.	
	25/5/17	5.30.	VII CORPS. M.G.O. gave lecture.	

T2134. Wt. W708–776. 500000. 4/15. Sir J. C. & S.

Instructions regarding War Diaries and Intelligence Summaries are contained in F. S. Regs., Part II. and the Staff Manual respectively. Title pages will be prepared in manuscript.

WAR DIARY
or
INTELLIGENCE SUMMARY.
(Erase heading not required.)

62 COMPANY.
MACHINE GUN CORPS.
Sheet 6.

Army Form C. 2118.

Place	Date	Hour	Summary of Events and Information	Remarks and references to Appendices
BLAIRVILLE	25/5/17 & 26/5/17	9 a.m	No 4 Section was attached to 12th NORTHd. Fus. and No 1 Section was attached to 13th NORTHd. Fus. for Tactical Scheme.	
"	27/5/17		TACTICAL EXERCISE by C.C for Officers of the Company. 2/LT. W. SMITH. 72 G.R.S joined for duty	
"	28/5/17	–	No 1 Section was attached to 13th NORTHd Fus. and No 3 Section was attached to 1st LINCOLN. Regt. for TACTICAL SCHEME. 1 N.C.O. proceeded to 21st DIVISIONAL SCHOOL for course of Gun Instruction.	
		2.30 p.m	Lecture given by G.O.C 21st DIVISION on "TACTICS."	
		5.30 p.m	Lecture given by VII Corps Intelligence Officer	
	29/5/17		LT. BOSWELL and 1 O.R. proceeded on leave to U.K.	
		5.30 p.m	Lecture by LT. PERKINS 62nd B.B.O. on "Bombs"	
"	30/5/17	2 p.m	Company marched from BLAIRVILLE to Railway Embankment at T. ~~27~~ 20.b.05.05 SHEET 51 B. S.W. 1/20,000 and bivouaced for the night.	
Railway Embankment	31/5/17	2.20 p.m	Company relieved the 100th M.G. Coy in the Hindenburgh line front extending from ... No 2 Section guns at T.11.d.9.6 T.11.d.9.7. T.11.d.9.8 T.11.d.9.9. No 3 Sections at U.13.b.4.7, U.13.d.95.70, U19.b.2.8, U19a.9.1. No 4 Sections at U.7.d.05.95, U.7.d.20.20, T18.b.6.3, U13.c.1.7. No 1 Section remaining in reserve at the Railway Embankment T.20.b.05.05. Company H.Q at Railway Embankment.	

Ends

W.B. Horsburgh Capt
Comndg 62 Company. M.G.C.

T2134. Wt. W708–776. 500000. 4/15. Sir J. C. & S.

Instructions regarding War Diaries and Intelligence Summaries are contained in F. S. Regs., Part II. and the Staff Manual respectively. Title Pages will be prepared in manuscript.

WAR DIARY
or
~~INTELLIGENCE SUMMARY~~
(Erase heading not required.)

62 COMPANY
MACHINE GUN CORPS.
Sheet I
Vol 16

Army Form C. 2118.

Place	Date	Hour	Summary of Events and Information	Remarks and references to Appendices
Nr ST. LEGER.	1/6/17.	11.15. a.m.	1 Gun, tripod and equipment for detachment blown to pieces by hostile shell fire at S.1. position U 19 b 30.80. 3 G.R. Wounded.	
		6.15 p.m.	Gun and team at S 2. U 19 a 90.10. buried by shell fire. No casualties, gun and all equipment recovered.	
"	2/6/17.		1 G.R. Killed 2 G.R.s wounded.	
			New disposition of Guns.	
			Front Line (1) U 7 c 95.95. (2) U 7 d 10.45 (3) U 13 b 40.70. (4) U 13 d 90.80.	
			Support Line (1) T 18 b. 60.30. (2) U 13 c 80.00. (3) U 13 a 20.10. (4) U 19 a 90.10.	
			Reserve Line (1) T 17 a 40.50. (2) T 18 c 30.45. (3) T 18 c 40.30.	
			3 Guns held in Company Reserve at T 11 d 50.60. 15 T 11 d 60.80. used for firing at back areas and suitable targets. Other Reserve positions at (1) T 22 d 40.20. (2) T 22 d 10.40. (3) T 22 d 00.80. (4) T 16 b 40.50.	
"	3/6/17		1 G.R. Wounded. 1 G.R. proceeded on Leave to U.K. No 1 Section moved to positions at (1) T 22 d 40.20. (2) T 22 d 10.40 (3) T 22 d 00.80. (4) T 16 b 40.50. During the night No 2 Sections guns fired 2000 rounds at Different points behind the enemies Lines.	

2449 Wt. W14957/M90 750,000 1/16 J.B.C. & A. Forms/C.2118/12.

Instructions regarding War Diaries and Intelligence Summaries are contained in F. S. Regs., Part II. and the Staff Manual respectively. Title Pages will be prepared in manuscript.

62 M.G Coy

Army Form C. 2118.

WAR DIARY

or

~~INTELLIGENCE SUMMARY~~

(Erase heading not required.)

Sheet II

Place	Date	Hour	Summary of Events and Information	Remarks and references to Appendices
Nr. St. LÉGER	4/6/17		a/CAPT. W. B. HORSBURGH, BEDFORD. REGT. to be CAPT. 3/2/17. (London Gazette 4/6/17).	
"	"	6.50pm	an enemy aeroplane was brought down near our gun position at U 19 a. 90.10. by one of our airmen. 150 rounds were fired at this aeroplane by No 1 Section.	
"	"		During the night 1500 rounds were fired at tracks behind enemies lines by No 2 Section.	
"	5/6/17		2000 Rounds were fired by No 2 Section at Targets behind enemies line.	
			Lt. C. J. Colley and 1 O.R. proceeded on leave to U. K.	
"	6/6/17		3 O.R.s wounded at Company Headquarters by explosion, caused by dropping an old piece of iron on the ground. (a Bosche Trap?) 1 O.R. proceeded to Rest Camp.	
"	7/6/17		Company relieved by 110 M. G. COMPANY. Relief Completed by 11 p.m. No Casualties.	
"			On completion of relief company marched to E CAMP. MOYENVILLE.	
			LT. TIPTAFT and 2 O.R. rejoined from Leave to U. K.	
			1 O.R. (driver) reported for duty from Base.	
MOYENVILLE	8/6/17.		Gun and equipment cleaned and overhauled.	
"	10/6/17		Lt. W. P. DEAN. and 1 O.R. proceeded to M. G. SCHOOL. CAMIERS. for "course of instruction"	

2449 Wt. W14957/M90 750,000 1/16 J.B.C. & A. Forms/C.2118/12.

62 M.G. COY.

Army Form C. 2118.

WAR DIARY
or
INTELLIGENCE SUMMARY

Sheet B

(Erase heading not required.)

Instructions regarding War Diaries and Intelligence Summaries are contained in F. S. Regs., Part II. and the Staff Manual respectively. Title Pages will be prepared in manuscript.

Place	Date	Hour	Summary of Events and Information	Remarks and references to Appendices
MOYENVILLE.	11/6/17.		2 O.R. rejoined from Base. 6 O.R. reported for duty from Base. Lt A. BIAGOTT. and 1 OR proceeded on Leave to U.K.	
"	12/6/17		Lt. J. BOSWELL rejoined from Leave to U.K.	
		6 p.m	Lecture given by G.O.C 21st DIVISIONAL ARTILLERY, on "The employment of artillery"	
		9 a.m.	Court of Enquiry held to investigate the accidental wounding of Ptes. ANDERSON. GRIFFITHS and GAGEN. President Lt J. DODSON. Members. LT. W.R TIPTAFT and 2/LT. G. LESLIE.	
"	15/6/17		1 O.R. proceeded to ABBEVILLE for "Transport Course."	
			2½ Sections (10 guns) attached to 110th Infantry Brigade to assist them in attack on HINDENBURG SUPPORT LINE (in front of FONTAINE-LES-CROISILLES) by overhead indirect fire and help to consolidate. 1 O.R wounded.	
	16/6/17.		1 O.R. killed 1 O.R. wounded.	
	17/6/17		1 O.R. proceeded on leave to U.K. 2½ Sections (10 guns) attached to 110 Infantry Brigade withdrawn from line and returned to E. CAMP. MOYENVILLE.	
"	18/6/17	11 a.m.	Company marched to BAILLEULVAL and went into billets.	

2449 Wt. W14957/M90 750,000 1/16 J.B.C. & A. Forms/C.2118/12.

62 M.G. Coy.

Army Form C. 2118.

Instructions regarding War Diaries and Intelligence Summaries are contained in F. S. Regs., Part II. and the Staff Manual respectively. Title Pages will be prepared in manuscript.

WAR DIARY
or
INTELLIGENCE SUMMARY

Sheet 4

(Erase heading not required.)

Place	Date	Hour	Summary of Events and Information	Remarks and references to Appendices
BAILLEULVAL.	19/6/17.	-	4 guns ~~and~~ No 3 Section under 2/LT. W. SMITH proceeded to SAULTY and relieved 4 guns of 100 M.G. Company for defence of dumps against hostile air craft. 2 G.R. proceeded on leave to U.K.	
"	22/6/17	-	No 3 Section (4 guns) withdrawn from SAULTY. 1 G.R. returned from Rest Camp. Sgt C J. CAINES. promoted Colour-Sgt. and transferred to 92 M.G. Company as C.Q.M.S.	
"	23/6/17	-	2/LT. W. SMITH. admitted to 3rd CANADIAN STATIONARY HOSPITAL. 1 G.R. proceeded to 3rd ARMY SCHOOL for course of COOKERY.	
"	24/6/17		LT C.J. COLLEY returned from leave. 2 G.R. proceeded to Rest Camp. 1 G.R. proceeded to M.G. School. CAMIERS.	
"	25/6/17		No 1 & No 2 Section fired Part I Table C. 28 G.R. inoculated T.A.B. LT. A. BIAGOTT returned from leave. No 3 & No 4 Section fired Part I Table C.	
"	26/6/17		23 G.R. inoculated T.A.B.	
"	29/6/17		Company entrained at BEAUMETZ and detrained at BOYELLES. and went into bivouac EAST of BOYELLES.	

2449 Wt. W14957/M90 750,000 1/16 J.B.C. & A. Forms/C.2118/12.

62 M. G. Company

Army Form C. 2118.

Instructions regarding War Diaries and Intelligence Summaries are contained in F. S. Regs., Part II. and the Staff Manual respectively. Title Pages will be prepared in manuscript.

WAR DIARY

~~or~~

~~INTELLIGENCE SUMMARY~~

(Erase heading not required.)

SHEET. V

Place	Date	Hour	Summary of Events and Information	Remarks and references to Appendices
BOYELLES	30-6-17	5-30am	Company relieved 98th M. G. Coy in the line. No 2 Section guns at U.1.c.3.5, U.1.c.15.10, U.1.c 85.20, in front line. Reserve No 4 Section. guns at T 10. D.3.3, T 11 a 2,4, T 11 a 2,5 T 4 b 80,35. No 1 & 3 Section remaining at BOYELLES in readiness to relieve the 150th M. G. Coy on the 1st July.	
			Ends	
			W.B. Horsburgh Capt. Commdg 62 Company Machine Gun Corps	

2449 Wt. W14957/M90 750,000 1/16 J.B.C. & A. Forms/C.2118/12.

Instructions regarding War Diaries and Intelligence Summaries are contained in F. S. Regs., Part II. and the Staff Manual respectively. Title pages will be prepared in manuscript.

WAR DIARY
or
INTELLIGENCE SUMMARY.
(Erase heading not required.)

SHEET. (I)

62 Company M.G.C.

Vol 17

Army Form C. 2118.

Place	Date	Hour	Summary of Events and Information	Remarks and references to Appendices
HINDERNBURGH LINE	1-7-17	/	Company relieved the 90th Company M.G.C in the HINDENBURGH LINE upon the Brigade extending their front.	
"			(I) Disposition of guns. Ref SHEETS. BULLECOURT. 1in10,000.	
"			Front line. F.4. O.31.c.80.00 F.3. T6.d.80.30. F.2. U.1.c.40.43.	
"			F.1. U.1.c. 88.14.	
"			Support line. S1. T.6.b.30.60. S2. T.6.b.05.57. S3 T.6.a.15.70.	
"			S4. M.36.c.50.57.	
"			Reserve line R.5. T.10.d.90.30. R.6 T.11.a.15.40 R7. T.11.a.15.50	
"			R8 T.4.b.80.45. R.9. M.35.b.80.85. and 3 guns in reserve at	
"			Company H.Q No 85 dugout Hindenburgh Support Trench.	
"			Lieut J. DODSON proceeded on leave to U.K. 1 O.R to M.G. School	
"			CAMIER. 1 OR admitted to F. Ambulance, and evac to C.C.S. struck off	
"			strength	
"	2-7-17	–	4 O.R joined from 41st M.G. Company and taken on strength of Coy	
			LT. DEAN & 2 OR rejoined from M.G SCHOOL, CAMIER.	
			2. O.R rejoined from leave.	

T2134. Wt. W708–776. 500000. 4/15. Sir J. C. & S.

Instructions regarding War Diaries and Intelligence Summaries are contained in F. S. Regs., Part II. and the Staff Manual respectively. Title pages will be prepared in manuscript.

WAR DIARY
or
INTELLIGENCE SUMMARY.
(Erase heading not required.)

62 Company M.G.C.

SHEET (II)

Army Form C. 2118.

Place	Date	Hour	Summary of Events and Information	Remarks and references to Appendices
HINDENBURGH	3-7-17		2 OR rejoined from leave.	
LINE	4-7-17		1 OR reported missing.	
H.Q. T.5.b.70.80	5-7-17		1 OR rejoined from Base.	
"	6-7-17		1 OR to Division Workshops for training as artificer.	
"	7-7-17		1 OR rejoined from HAMELINCOURT.	
"	8-7-17		LIEUT BIAGOTT relieves Capt HORSBURGH in the line. Capt HORSBURGH	
"	"		returning to the transport lines, BOYELLES.	
"	"		2 OR to Rest Camp.	
"	9-7-17		2 OR joined from Base, LIEUT STEPHENSON joined from Base, 1 OR	
"			rejoined and taken on strength.	
"	10-7-17		Capt HORSBURGH proceeded on leave to U.K. Lieut BIAGOTT assumed	
"	"		command of the company. Lieut STEPHENSON took command of No 3	
"			Section in the line.	
"	11-7-17	9-30pm	Indirect fire opened on enemy working parties in front of our	
"			posts and good results obtained. firing continued for 4 hours.	
"	12-7-17		1 OR wounded and evacuated to C.C.S. Indirect fire opened on	

Instructions regarding War Diaries and Intelligence Summaries are contained in F. S. Regs., Part II. and the Staff Manual respectively. Title pages will be prepared in manuscript.

WAR DIARY
or
INTELLIGENCE SUMMARY.
(Erase heading not required.)

62 Company M.G.C.

SHEET (3)

Army Form C. 2118.

Place	Date	Hour	Summary of Events and Information	Remarks and references to Appendices
HINDENBURGH	12-7-17	9-30p	enemy working parties until dawn 13th. 5,000 rounds fired.	
LINE	13-7-17		Lines of fire of F3 & F1 altered to. M.G.F3 firing at German Front line	
HQ T.5.b.70.85	13-7-17		from U.7.d.50.75 to U.7.d.80.50. M.G.F1. firing down German Front Trench	
"	"		at 157° True Bearing.	
	14-7-17		2/Lieut LESLIE & 1OR proceeded on leave to U.K. Lieut DODSON	
	"		rejoined from leave.	
"	"		Indirect Fire carried out during the night at enemy working	
"	"		parties and tracks behind the Enemys Support Line. 10,000 rounds fired	
"	15-7-17		Indirect fire carried out at tracks leading to Enemy Support Trench	
"	"		and at Enemy Working Parties on their wire.	
"	16-7-17	12 noon	Company relieved in the line by the 64th Company M.G.C.	
"	"		No 9 Section marched to CROISELLES and took over the Posts. C1 to	
"	"		C5 for Anti aircraft defence from the 64th Company M.G.C.	
MOYONVILLE	"	4pm	Remainder of Company marched back to the Rest Camp MOYONVILLE	
"	"		2 guns mounted just outside the Camp MOYONVILLE against hostile	
"	"		aircraft.	
	"			

T2134. Wt. W708-776. 500000. 4/15. Sir J. C. & S.

Instructions regarding War Diaries and Intelligence Summaries are contained in F. S. Regs., Part II. and the Staff Manual respectively. Title Pages will be prepared in manuscript.

WAR DIARY
or
INTELLIGENCE SUMMARY

(Erase heading not required.)

62 Company M. G. C.

SHEET (4)

Army Form C. 2118.

Place	Date	Hour	Summary of Events and Information	Remarks and references to Appendices
MOYONVILLE	17-7-17	9am	Cleaning up of men and personal kit. Inspection of same by Section	
"			Officers 2 pm.	
"	18-7-17	9am	General clean up of guns & equipment and checking of same.	
"		12 noon	Repacking of limbers. Lt CLARKE H W joined from Base.	
"	19-7-17	4pm	No 3 Section relieved at CROISELLES by 1 Section of the	
"	"		237th Company M. G. C. and joined the remainder of Coy at MOYONVILLE.	
"	"		Lt DODSON & Lt TIPTAFT leave to AMIENS. 3 OR Etc.	
"	20-7-17		Lecture on Cooking at D Camp the O.C and 5 O.R attending.	
"	"		LT. BOSWELL & LT COLLEY 3 OR leave to AMIENS.	
"	22-7-17		2 OR to Rest Camp St VALERY SUR SOMME. 2 OR rejoined from	
"			same.	
"	23-7-17		Capt HORSBURGH rejoined from leave and assumed command of	
			the Company.	
HINDENBURGH LINE. HQ T 5.b. 80.75.	24-7-17	11am	Company relieved the 64th Company M.G.C. in the line Left Sector Div Front.	

2449 Wt. W14957/M90 750,000 1/16 J.B.C. & A. Forms/C.2118/12.

Instructions regarding War Diaries and Intelligence Summaries are contained in F. S. Regs., Part II. and the Staff Manual respectively. Title Pages will be prepared in manuscript.

WAR DIARY
or
INTELLIGENCE SUMMARY

(Erase heading not required.)

62 Company M.G.C.

SHEET (5)

Army Form C. 2118.

Place	Date	Hour	Summary of Events and Information	Remarks and references to Appendices
HINDENBURGH	24-7-17	11am	Disposition of guns. Front line guns. position LF1. U1c 90,20. LF2. V1c. 40,50	
LINE. Coy	"		LF3. T6d. 90,35. L.F.4. U1a. 80,95.	
H.Q.	"		New Support line guns LS1. T.6.b. 10,60. LS.2. T6b.25,70.	
T5b.80,75.	"		Intermediate line guns. LI.1. T11d.89,80. LI.2. T5d 70,70. LI.3. T6a 20,80.	
"	"		LI.4. N36c.55,45. LI 5 N35b.80,20.	
"	"		Reserve line gun. R9. T5a.45,90. & 4 guns in reserve at Coy HQ.	
"	"		LF3. fired at target U7d.6.8 during the night 24th 25th.	
"	25-7-17		L.F.1 and L.F.3 fired on SOS line to verify Trajectory Clearance over own	
"	"		troops on Lump Lane in Right Sector.	
"	"		2 OR proceeded on leave to U.K.	
"	27-7-17		The following areas of ground were fired on during the night 27-28th	
"	"		to protect work to be carried out by the 1st LINCOLNS & 10th YORKS Regts	
"	"		U1b.60,60, U1b.75,20. U1d 75,95. U2c.05,60. U2a.00,50 and all	
"	"		FONTAINE WOOD. U2a.	
"	"		1 O.R. joined from the 110th Company M.G.C.	

2449 Wt. W14957/M90 750,000 1/16 J.B.C. & A. Forms/C.2118/12.

Instructions regarding War Diaries and Intelligence Summaries are contained in F. S. Regs., Part II. and the Staff Manual respectively. Title pages will be prepared in manuscript.

WAR DIARY
or
INTELLIGENCE SUMMARY.
(Erase heading not required.) SHEET. (6)

62 Company M.G.C.

Army Form C. 2118.

Place	Date	Hour	Summary of Events and Information	Remarks and references to Appendices
Coy H.Q.	28-7-17		Raid carried out by the 1st LINCOLNS REGT on Enemy Gun emplacement	
T5b 80,75	"		U1b, 70,60. LI 3 fired on objective at intervals from Dusk to ZERO – 15 min	
"	"		The following guns fired on selected targets from Zero to Zero + 30 mins	
"			maintaining continuous fire.	
"	"		LF 3 target U1d 75,95, LF.4. U1b ~~70,20~~ 80,70, Reserve gun at T.6b 40,05	
"	"		target U1b. 70,20. on the night 28th 29th, Zero 1-30 am.	
"	"		LI.1 target U1d 95,60. LI 2. target U2c. 10,15. LI 4 U1d, 45,60.	
"	"		2OR to M.G School on course, 2OR leave to U.K.	
"	29-7-17		1O.R rejoined from leave. 1OR. course from M.G School.	
"	"		LI 3. fired at intervals during the night 29.30th, target U1b 70,05.	
"	"		Reserve gun at T.6b. 40,05 at target U1b. 75,35.	
"	30-7-17		1OR transferred to M.G. Bn.	
"	"		10th YORKSHIRE Regt raided an enemy strong point on the night 30,31st objective	
"	"		at U1d 75,95. (a) a reserve gun in SHAFT TRENCH fired on the objective	
"	"		from dusk to ZERO – 15 minutes, small bursts at frequent intervals.	
"	"		(B) LI 3 fired on FONTAINE WOOD between ZERO – 30 minutes and ZERO.	

T2134. Wt. W708–776. 500000. 4/15. Sir J. C. & S.

Instructions regarding War Diaries and Intelligence Summaries are contained in F. S. Regs., Part II. and the Staff Manual respectively. Title pages will be prepared in manuscript.

WAR DIARY
or
INTELLIGENCE SUMMARY.
(Erase heading not required.)

62 Company
M.G.C.
SHEET (7)

Army Form C. 2118.

Place	Date	Hour	Summary of Events and Information	Remarks and references to Appendices
Company H.Q.	30-7-17	–	in order to drown the sound of the party.	
I.5.b. 80,75	"		(C) The following guns fired on selected areas. 4 Reserve guns at	
"	"		I 6 b 30,10. LF 4. LI 3, & LI 4. rate of fire:- from ZERO to ZERO +	
"	"		10 minutes, 100 rounds per gun per minute. From Zero + 10 to Zero + 20 minutes	
"	"		200 rounds per gun per minute. & from Zero + 20 min to Zero + 40 min	
"	"		50 rounds per gun per minute. (Zero 2 am.)	
"	31-7-17		1 OR to ABBEVILLE on Farriery course.	
	"		L.I.3 Gun fired on FONTAINE WOOD in U2 a. during night of	
			31.7.17 – 1.8.17. from 10.30pm to 2.30 am. (bursts of 30-50 rounds	
			at intervals of 2-7 minutes.)	
			Ends	
			W. B. Horsbrugh. Capt	
			O.C. 62 Company	
			M.G.C.	

(A7092). Wt. W12839/M1293. 75,000. 1/17. D. D. & L., Ltd. Forms/C.2118/14.

Instructions regarding War Diaries and Intelligence Summaries are contained in F. S. Regs., Part II. and the Staff Manual respectively. Title pages will be prepared in manuscript.

WAR DIARY
or
~~INTELLIGENCE~~ SUMMARY.
(Erase heading not required.)

62 Company M.G.C

SHEET (I)

Army Form C. 2118.

Vol 18

Place	Date	Hour	Summary of Events and Information	Remarks and references to Appendices
			Reference MAP. 51b. S.W.	
HINDENBURG	1-8-17	1-3am	The following guns opened fire (indirect) at the following targets	
LINE	"		L13. T6b.04 target U1D.70,95 to U2c10,50. U2a 4,50, U1a 55,60	
Company H.Q	"		traversing 1° right. Rate of fire 30 to 50 rounds at about 3 minute	
T5b.79,80	"		interval	
"	"		2OR killed 1OR wounded	
"	3-8-17	1-30am	M.G. L13 opened indirect fire on enemy targets at U1D95,60	
"	"		to U2c30,50. 30 to 50 rounds at 3 minute interval.	
"	"	3-30am	Reserve Gun at T6b15,25 opened fire at targets U2d.10,20 to 2°	
"	"	"	right & left. 50 rounds at intervals of 3 minutes.	
"	4-8-17	"	5 O.R. joined from Base and taken on strength of the company.	
"	5-8-17	1-30am	Indirect fire opened on to enemy targets during the night.	
"	"		Lieut W DEAN & 1OR proceeded on leave to U.K. 2OR rejoined from	
"	"		Rest Camp. 2 OR proceeded to Rest Camp.	
"	6-8-17		Readjustment of the Divisional Front. Left Brigade Front. 62nd	
"	"		Infantry Brigade. Left Boundary North of the line Pug LANE	
"	"		SHAFT TRENCH to its junction with BROWN TRENCH thence through	

T2134. Wt. W708-776. 500000. 4/15. Sir J. C. & S.

Instructions regarding War Diaries and Intelligence Summaries are contained in F. S. Regs., Part II. and the Staff Manual respectively. Title pages will be prepared in manuscript.

WAR DIARY
or
INTELLIGENCE SUMMARY.
(Erase heading not required.)

62 Company M.G.C.

SHEET (2)

Army Form C. 2118.

Place	Date	Hour	Summary of Events and Information	Remarks and references to Appendices
HINDENBURG LINE Coy HQ T5 b 70.80	6-8-17		Southern extremity of FOULDNER LANE to T5 Central thence due	
	"		WEST, S of HENIN.	
	"		Right Brigade Boundary. Junction of NELLY LANE and BURG TRENCH	
	"		Junction of FACTORY and GUARDIAN TRENCH thence to SE corner	
	"		of ST LEGER WOOD.	
	"	3 pm	<u>DISPOSITION of GUNS</u> <u>FRONT LINE</u> W13 b 47,00, W 7c 99,95, 2 guns.	
	"		W1c 90,25, W1c 35,50. T6d 70,40. <u>SUPPORT LINE</u> U 13a 20,15. T 18b 50,30.	
	"		T6b 10,60. <u>INTEMEDIATE LINE</u> T 11d 75,00. T11d 80,40. T5d 70,70.	
	"		<u>RESERVE</u> 1 Section at the Railway Embankment ST LEGER T20d.	
	7-8-17		2 OR rejoined from leave. 1 OR evacuated sick to C.C.S. LIEUT. LESLIE	"
	"		rejoined from leave.	
"	8-8-17		1 OR joined from 151 Company M.G.C.	
"	9-8-17	2 pm	Company relieved in the line by the 237 Company M.G.C. and	
			marched back by Section to E CAMP. MOYONVILLE. Relief	
			complete 12 midnight.	
			1 OR rejoined from leave.	

T2134. Wt. W708-776. 500000. 4/15. Sir J. C. & S.

Instructions regarding War Diaries and Intelligence Summaries are contained in F. S. Regs., Part II. and the Staff Manual respectively. Title pages will be prepared in manuscript.

WAR DIARY
or
INTELLIGENCE SUMMARY.
(Erase heading not required.)

62 Company M.G.C.

SHEET (3)

Army Form C. 2118.

Place	Date	Hour	Summary of Events and Information	Remarks and references to Appendices
E. CAMP MOYONVILLE	10-8-17	9am	1 OR (wounded) rejoined from Base, 1 OR rejoined from leave.	
"			General clean up of personal equipment and gun gear	
"	11-8-17		8 OR proceeded on leave to U.K.	
"	to		Systematical training carried out during this period.	
"	15-8-17		" " " " " "	
"	16-8-17		2/Lieut TILLOTSON H. proceeded on leave to UK	
NEW CAMP	17-8-17		Company relieved 110 Company M.G.C. in the New Camp MOYONVILLE	
MOYONVILLE	"	4pm	No 1 & 3 Sections relieved 2 Sections of the 110 M.G. Coy in	
"	"		Reserve Positions at the Railway Embankment T24 d to U25 a	
"	"		and U25 b.	
"	"		No 1 Section in positions M.G.R.I.3, RI.4, RI.5, RI.6. Targets U21 d 70.45	
"	"		U21 d 5.5, U7 d 75.15, U7 d 7.4.	
"	"		No 3 Section M.G.R.I.7. RI.8. LI.1, LI.2. Targets U7 b. 7.4.	
"	"		U20 b 8.7, (OLDENBURGH LANE U8 a 15.10) U14 a 14.45.	
"	"		No 2 & 4 Sections remaining at MOYONVILLE	
"	18-8-17		6 O.R. proceeded on leave to UK.	
"	"			

T2134. Wt. W708-776. 500000. 4/15. Sir J. C. & S.

Instructions regarding War Diaries and Intelligence Summaries are contained in F. S. Regs., Part II. and the Staff Manual respectively. Title pages will be prepared in manuscript.

WAR DIARY
or
INTELLIGENCE SUMMARY.
(Erase heading not required.)

62 Company M.G.C.

SHEET (4)

Army Form C. 2118.

Place	Date	Hour	Summary of Events and Information	Remarks and references to Appendices
NEW CAMP MOYONVILLE	19-8-17		2 OR rejoined from Rest Camp. 2 OR proceeded to Rest Camp.	
"	20-8-17		1 OR evacuated & Struck off strength. 1 OR leave to U.K.	
"	21-8-17	4 pm	No 2 & 4 Sections relieved Nos 1 & 3 Sections at the Railway	
"	"		Embankment. No 1 & 3 Sections returning to MOYONVILLE.	
"	22-8-17		No 1 Section took up the following positions for barrage work	
"	"		on a Brigade of Artillery being withdrawn. Along the Railway	
"	"		Embankment U 25 a & U 26 c. firing at U 14 central, U 21 a &	
"	"		U 20 c	
"	"		Capt W. B. HORSBURGH proceeded to Small Arms School G.H.Q.	
"	"		and 1 OR ditto.	
"	23-8-17		Lieut CHALMERS from 28 Company M.G.C. assumed command of	
"			the company. 1 OR joined from 28th M.G Coy (Servant)	
"	24-8-17		10 O.R joined from Base. 1 OR admitted to C.C.S.	
"	25-8-17		No 2 Section relieved from Reserve Position R17, R18, R19	
"	"		& L.I.1. by 1 Section of the 48th Company M.G.C. After relief No 2	
"	"		Section marched back to MOYONVILLE	

T2134. Wt. W708–776. 500000. 4/15. Sir J. C. & S.

Instructions regarding War Diaries and Intelligence Summaries are contained in F. S. Regs., Part II. and the Staff Manual respectively. Title pages will be prepared in manuscript.

WAR DIARY
or
INTELLIGENCE SUMMARY.
(Erase heading not required.)

62 Company M.G.C.

SHEET (5)

Army Form C. 2118.

Place	Date	Hour	Summary of Events and Information	Remarks and references to Appendices
MOYONVILLE	25-8-17	2 pm	2 OR proceeded to Base and struck off strength of company.	
"	26-8-17		8 OR proceeded on leave to U.K. 1 OR joined from Base.	
"	"	10 am	Transport moved from ERVILLERS and marched to the NEW	
"	"		CAMP MOYONVILLE.	
"	"		No 4 Section relieved from the Reserve Positions at RI.3.	
"	"		RI.4. RI.5. RI.6. by 1 section of the 43rd Company M.G.C	
"	"		after relief No 4 Section marched back to MOYONVILLE	
"	"		LIEUT W DEAN struck off the strength of the company. Medical	
"	"		Board ordered in U.K. (War Office daily letter).	
"	27-8-17		No 2 section withdrawn from special barrage position along	
"	"		Railway Embankment, and marched back to MOYONVILLE	
"	"		~~7 OR proceeded on leave to U.K~~	
MOYONVILLE	28-8-17	10-30	Company paraded and marched to new area and billeted in	
			DAINVILLE at 2 pm.	
DAINVILLE	29-8-17		General clean up of gun gear, personal equipment. Etc.	
			1 officer & 2 OR attend lecture on "Lewis Gun firing [illegible]	

T2134. Wt. W708–776. 500000. 4/15. Sir J. C. & S.

Instructions regarding War Diaries and Intelligence Summaries are contained in F. S. Regs., Part II. and the Staff Manual respectively. Title pages will be prepared in manuscript.

WAR DIARY or ~~INTELLIGENCE SUMMARY.~~

(Erase heading not required.)

Army Form C. 2118.

62 Company M.G.C.

SHEET (6)

Place	Date	Hour	Summary of Events and Information	Remarks and references to Appendices
			Ref MAP 51c N.E.	
DAINVILLE	29-8-17		Nil.	
"	30/8/17		Company instructed in MACHINE GUN BARRAGE at training area near WAILLY. Lt. A. BIAGOTT proceeded on leave to U.K. 2/LT. H. TILLOTSON rejoined from leave. LT. J. BOSWELL and 2.O.R proceeded to MACHINE GUN SCHOOL CAMIERS for course of instruction.	
"	31/8/17		Company instructed in MACHINE GUN BARRAGE at training area near WAILLY. 1 Officer and 2 N.C.O.s attended demonstration of the use of the UKON PACK at BERNVILLE. 2	
		2.30 pm	Lecture by MAJOR. BOWDEN. O.C. 110 M.G. COMPANY on "MACHINE GUN BARRAGE". 4 O.R. rejoined from leave.	

Ends.

J. Chalmers Captain,
Comdg. 62 M.G. Coy.

T2134. Wt. W708–776. 500000. 4/15. Sir J. C. & S.

Instructions regarding War Diaries and Intelligence Summaries are contained in F. S. Regs., Part II. and the Staff Manual respectively. Title pages will be prepared in manuscript.

WAR DIARY
or
INTELLIGENCE SUMMARY.
(Erase heading not required.)

Army Form C. 2118.

62nd Coy M.G. Corps

(1.)

Vol 19

Place	Date	Hour	Summary of Events and Information	Remarks and references to Appendices
DAINVILLE.	1/9/17.	–	Section inspections at 8.45 a.m. The forenoon (9am – 1pm) was devoted to preparation for barrage scheme arranged by D.M.G.O. Dug trenches on WAILLY training area. Put in platforms for guns under ground level & cut barrage slots. Laid telephone wire for control of batteries in conjunction with 64th Coy. & 237th (Divisional) Coy. Two teams of No. 4 Section relieved two teams of 4th Div. on Anti-Aircraft duty at ANZIN. Weather better but still broken.	
	2/9/17.	–	Coy. attended Divine Service. The parade was well turned out. Devoted the day to office work. Made arrangements for reorganisation of Transport. Inspected the billets & camp area; found them clean but untidy. Issued orders accordingly. Had camouflages prepared for next day's barrage scheme. Carried out experiments with Anti-Aircraft fitting supplied for adjustment to MK. 4 tripod. 1 Officer proceeded to rest camp.	
	3/9/17	–	Paraded to proceed to training area at 8.30 am. Completed digging & camouflaging of barrage positions. Carried out practice S.O.S. & concentration in conjunction with 64th & 237th Coys. Afternoon was devoted to recreation; weather good & all ranks in excellent spirits. 7 O.R. proceeded to U.K. on furlough.	
	4/9/17	–	Section inspections at 8.45 a.m. Barrage drill practised during the morning.	

(A7092). Wt. W12839/M1293. 75,0.0. 1/17. D. D. & L., Ltd. Forms/C.2118/14.

Instructions regarding War Diaries and Intelligence Summaries are contained in F. S. Regs., Part II. and the Staff Manual respectively. Title pages will be prepared in manuscript.

WAR DIARY
or
INTELLIGENCE SUMMARY.
(Erase heading not required.)

Army Form C. 2118.

Place	Date	Hour	Summary of Events and Information	Remarks and references to Appendices
DAINVILLE	4/9/17 (contd.)	–	Sent party to range to work on emplacements. Bathing during the afternoon; cricket & football practices organised by officers. Inspected work on training area during the evening. 1 Officer to hospital for dental treatment.	
	5/9/17	–	Coy. paraded at 8.30 a.m. & proceeded to range. Practised laying out lines of fire, distributing for S.O.S. & concentrating on given targets. The day was excellent & all ranks worked well. Coy. Commanders' conference with D.M.G.O. in view of demonstration of barrage fire & battery control to be given on the 6th inst. Arrangements [illegible]. Extended the 'phone system employed for the batteries & placed the screen required for safety during the practice. Returned to billets at 2 p.m. & devoted afternoon to cricket match v. T. M. B. in the Brigade Competition. The Coy. won the match.	
	6/9/17	–	Coy. paraded at 8.30 a.m. & marched to training area. Battery in position by 9.45 a.m.; screen posted, & 'phone system established by 10 a.m. Inspected by Divisional General & Staff Officers & senior battalion commanders at 10.30 a.m. Showed the battery in action at 11 a.m. & carried out demonstration of S.O.S., box barrage & concentration between	

(A7092). Wt. W12839/M1293 75,000. 1/17. D. D. & L., Ltd. Forms/C.2118/14.

Instructions regarding War Diaries and Intelligence Summaries are contained in F. S. Regs., Part II. and the Staff Manual respectively. Title pages will be prepared in manuscript.

WAR DIARY
or
INTELLIGENCE SUMMARY.
(Erase heading not required.)

Army Form C. 2118.

Place	Date	Hour	Summary of Events and Information	Remarks and references to Appendices
DAINVILLE	6/9/17	(contd.)	12 noon + 12.45 pm. The whole demonstration was completely successful, the firing being very accurate as witnessed by the hits obtained on the targets set out. Returned to camp at 2 pm. + devoted afternoon to recreation. Thunder during evening; heavy rains, but billets kept dry + comfortable. Special Divisional letter received stating G.O.Cs. appreciation of demonstration carried out in the morning.	
	7/9/17	–	Inspected the Company at 9.15 am. Found all ranks well equipped but deficient in detail. Slackness noticeable in repairing of clothes + indenting of replacements. Inspected Transport. Found harness good, repairs well up to date + all limbers in sound condition. Shoeing showed room for improvement. Personnel slack in detail + require careful supervision. Inspected gun stores + found them in good condition. Inspected the sections in gun drill. The men were slow + inaccurate; they need practice + plenty of drill to bring them up to standard. Bathing + pay parades during the afternoon. Received preliminary orders in view of probable	

(A7092). Wt. W12839/M1293. 750,000. 1/17. D. D. & L., Ltd. Forms/C.2118/14.

Instructions regarding War Diaries and Intelligence Summaries are contained in F. S. Regs., Part II. and the Staff Manual respectively. Title pages will be prepared in manuscript.

WAR DIARY
or
INTELLIGENCE SUMMARY.
(Erase heading not required.)

Army Form C. 2118.

(4)

Place	Date	Hour	Summary of Events and Information	Remarks and references to Appendices
DAINVILLE	7/9/17 (contd.)		move of half company on the 8th inst. to 10th Corps area & made necessary preliminary arrangements.	
"	8/9/17	–	Sixty O.R. paraded at 8.45am. & proceeded to new area. The O.C. & the section officers accompanied this party leaving the balance of the Coy. under the actg. 2nd i/c. Advance party proceeded by bus to ST. POL where convoy with 64th, 110th & 237th Coys. was completed at 11am. Proceeded via HAZEBROOK & ABEELE to No. 2 Camp DICKEBUSH. Arrived 6/pm. Drew bivouacs & tents & pitched camp. All ranks bivouaced & under cover by 10pm. Balance of Coy. had general parades under 2nd i/c at DAINVILLE.	
DICKEBUSH	9/9/17	–	Rearranged camp, dressed bivouacs, dug drainage etc. Received preliminary orders from D.M.G.O. 41st Div. to which Division this detachment of the Coy. was now attached for operations. The vicinity of the camp was bombed during the day. Made reconnaissance of proposed battery positions this afternoon & evening. These positions were about six miles from camp. No guides provided or conveyance arranged. Had a party of 26 O.R. up as far as LARCH WOOD by 7pm.	BELGIUM & FRANCE SHEET 28. I29.c

(A7092). Wt. W12839/M1293 75,000. 1/17. D. D. & L., Ltd. Forms/C.2118/14

Instructions regarding War Diaries and Intelligence Summaries are contained in F. S. Regs., Part II. and the Staff Manual respectively. Title pages will be prepared in manuscript.

WAR DIARY
or
INTELLIGENCE SUMMARY.
(*Erase heading not required.*)

Army Form C. 2118.

Place	Date	Hour	Summary of Events and Information	Remarks and references to Appendices
DICKEBUSH.	9/9/17	(contd.)	but owing to absence of guides etc. only succeeded in making a dump of tools. Party returned to camp at 10 p.m. Gas shell alarm at midnight.	
"	10/9/17	–	Round line with D.M.G.O. 41st Div. Located battery positions carefully with a view to calculations. Arranged for lorries to take the working party to the line every night. Arranged for ammn. supply. Selected Groups Hqs. Battery Hqs. Belt filling depots etc. Returned to camp at 4 pm. First fatigue of 1 off. + 20 O.R. left by lorries at 6 pm. Camp improved during the day, mess + cookhouses, latrines etc. Air raid to N. + W. of camp at 9.15 pm. Aerial activity throughout the day. The ground proved difficult, the approach to positions being exposed + under continuous field gun fire. Weather was good. In the Divisional M.G. Drill competition held near DAINVILLE the company secured first place.	
"	11/9/17	–	Fatigue party to trenches. Cleared belt filling depots + dug ammn. recesses. One O.R. was wounded. Gas shells hindered work during the night. Fine weather continued resulting in great aerial activity throughout the day. Enemy aircraft were active over the camp at night.	

(A7092). Wt. W12839/M1293 75,000. 1/17. D. D. & L., Ltd. Forms/C.2118/14

Instructions regarding War Diaries and Intelligence Summaries are contained in F. S. Regs., Part II. and the Staff Manual respectively. Title pages will be prepared in manuscript.

WAR DIARY
or
INTELLIGENCE SUMMARY.
(Erase heading not required.)

(6.)

Army Form C. 2118.

Place	Date	Hour	Summary of Events and Information	Remarks and references to Appendices
DICKEBUSH	12/9/17	–	Accompanied D.M.G.O. 21st Div round Group positions + settled details of communication etc. Enemy light guns were active. The preparations for attack on our whole front in this area seemed obvious. Working party proceeded to line as usual & carried up 3 baby elephants, dug further ammn recesses + cleaned out two more belt filling depots. Enemy counter battery work was very good throughout the day. Rain threatened towards night but did not hinder work.	
"	13/9/17	–	Visited battery positions during the morning + inspected the work which had made satisfactory progress. Reported to Adv. Div. Hq. at 6pm for instructions. Fatigue to line at 5pm: put in 4 more baby elephants + worked on left battery positions. Work was hindered by rain, + by heavy shelling during the night.	
"	14/9/17	–	Worked out calculations for switches during the forthcoming operations + submitted same to D.M.G.O. Weather improved + good progress made with work. Four more elephants put in + right battery positions completed. Great aerial activity throughout the day.	
"	15/9/17	–	Operation Orders received. O.C. Coy. conference with D.M.G.O. re operations. Whole detachment carried up ammunition at night. 350,000 rds. put in for this group. Fatigues from 237 + 238 Coys. supplied to assist in the work. There was a marked increase in artillery activity.	
"	16/9/17	–	Submitted calculations for barrages as laid down in operation orders. Enemy air reconnaissance in force (14 machines) at 11 am. One officer	

(A7092). Wt. W12839/M1293 75,000. 1/17. D. D. & L., Ltd. Forms/C.2118/14.

Instructions regarding War Diaries and Intelligence Summaries are contained in F. S. Regs., Part II. and the Staff Manual respectively. Title pages will be prepared in manuscript.

WAR DIARY
or
INTELLIGENCE SUMMARY.
(Erase heading not required.)

Army Form C. 2118.

(7.)

Place	Date	Hour	Summary of Events and Information	Remarks and references to Appendices
DICKEBUSH	16/9/17	(contd.)	and 1 O.R. proceeded to CASSEL to meet remainder of Company due ~~there at~~ 10 p.m. No working party sent to line, all ranks being given a nights rest. Drew bivouacs & tents & prepared camp for arrival of company.	
"	17/9/17	–	Personnel from CASSEL arrived with [illegible] by bus at 3 am. Transport followed by route march arriving at 1 p.m. Received orders at 11 am to move a section to the line to conduct practice barrages. Warned No 1 & worked out necessary calculations, & made arrangements for all belt boxes to go in & petrol tins with reserve water. No 1 Section entrained at 5 pm & carrying party followed at 6.30 pm. Had section inspection of anti gas appliances, iron rations & field dressings. Cleaned all gun gear & ammunition. No. 1 Sect. had two casualties going into position. Received orders to change barrage lines. Worked new calculations accordingly. Issued Operation Orders. Weather conditions still favourable	APPENDIX "A"
"	18/9/17	–	D.M.G.O. addressed the Company on forthcoming operation. Officers conference followed to discuss details. Battery commanders with gun commanders & Nos. 1 & 2 went up to positions. No 1 Section carried out practice barrages at 6 am & 8.30 pm. Slight casualties during the night from these fire.	

(A7092). Wt. W12839/M1293 75,000. 1/17. D. D. & L., Ltd. Forms/C.2118/14.

Instructions regarding War Diaries and Intelligence Summaries are contained in F. S. Regs., Part II. and the Staff Manual respectively. Title pages will be prepared in manuscript.

WAR DIARY
or
INTELLIGENCE SUMMARY.
(Erase heading not required.)

Army Form C. 2118.

(8)

Place	Date	Hour	Summary of Events and Information	Remarks and references to Appendices
IN THE LINE	19/9/17	–	Moved to Group Hq at junction of CLONMEL COPSE & SHREWSBURY FOREST at 9.30 am. Work of preparation completed throughout the day. Right battery co-operated in practice barrage at 3pm. Left battery position already seemed unfortunate being apparently just within enemy barrage line. Right battery had no trouble. Enemy aircraft active throughout the day. Received notification of ZERO hour at 7pm. Nos. 3 & 4 for the guns reported at 8pm. 2/Lt Tillotson who was in charge of this party did not report.	SHEET 28
"	20/9/17	–	The night was comparatively quiet. Group reported ready at 5.30am. Enemy had been fairly active for an hour. The rain which had been heavy during the night cleared off before ZERO leaving the ground damp but conditions otherwise good. Barrage opened punctually at ZERO hour (5.40 am). The need of efficient N.C.O.s was apparent from the start to relieve the battery officers of detail. Guns fired well & the barrage was steadily kept up & lifted to second line on time. There was no difficulty in this. Went round all guns at 9am. All ranks had settled down to steady work at their various duties, work [illegible] was proceeding well & the ammn. supply being kept well in hand. Gunners were firing & laying excellently. The batteries were	

(A7092). Wt. W12839/M1293. 750,000. 1/17. D. D. & L., Ltd. Forms/C.2118/14.

WAR DIARY
or
INTELLIGENCE SUMMARY.
(Erase heading not required.)

Army Form C. 2118.

Instructions regarding War Diaries and Intelligence Summaries are contained in F. S. Regs., Part II. and the Staff Manual respectively. Title pages will be prepared in manuscript.

(9.)

Place	Date	Hour	Summary of Events and Information	Remarks and references to Appendices
IN THE LINE	20/9/17	(Contd)	not too much worried by enemy shelling although the left battery again found itself in a barrage & suffered further casualties. The operations of the infantry seemed successful judging by the numbers of prisoners being brought back. By 10 am. enemy shelling had quite lifted from the area of the Batteries & was now much further forward. Enemy aircraft now became active flying well back over our lines. Received orders for concentration at 11.30 am. The group was in action at 11.32 am. Fired 10 minutes rapid & ten slow. Stood by for S.O.S. till 5 pm. when orders were received for shoot at 6.30 pm. in support of 122 & 123 Brigades who attacked the strong point still holding out in the Green Line. Carried out shoot accordingly. At 7.15 pm. S.O.S. went up on the right & then in front. Group opened up rapid, continued after five minutes at medium rate for 20 minutes, then slackened till 7.55 pm when situation was again normal. Received orders at 11 pm. to carry out harassing fire throughout the night. Accordingly two guns of right battery fired intermittently till 3 am. & two guns left battery from 3 am. till 6 am. The night was marked by spasmodic shelling by the enemy & steady bombardment by our	

Instructions regarding War Diaries and Intelligence Summaries are contained in F. S. Regs., Part II. and the Staff Manual respectively. Title pages will be prepared in manuscript.

WAR DIARY
or
INTELLIGENCE SUMMARY.

(Erase heading not required.)

(10.)

Army Form C. 2118.

Place	Date	Hour	Summary of Events and Information	Remarks and references to Appendices
IN THE LINE	20/9/17	–	own artillery. Conditions remained favourable. Lt. Fillotson reported having been stunned by a shell the previous night.	
"	21/9/17	–	S.O.S. by 'plane at 4.30 am. Answered within one minute & continued to fire at decreasing rate till 5 am. Lt. Tipsett killed at 5.35 am. There were three other casualties. Three guns were also put out of action. Received orders at 6.30 am re proposed attack on remaining portion of Green Line at 9.30 am. Arranged fire programme accordingly. Great aerial activity throughout the morning but position otherwise quiet. Conditions remained favourable & shoot was fired as arranged. Stood by for S.O.S. throughout the day men not on sentry being fully employed cleaning guns & filling belts. Concentration switch ordered at 4.25 pm. followed by shoot on S.O.S. lines which lasted till 5 pm. These shoots were ordered by D.M.G.O. & communicated by 'phone. S.O.S. by signal at 6.58 pm. Batteries got on at once. Slackened off at 7.20 pm. & continued medium & slow till 7.40 pm. Another gun was put out of action. Angles of distribution were altered to keep the front covered when guns became casualties.	

(A7092). Wt. W12839/M1293. 75,000. 1/17. D. D. & L., Ltd. Forms/C.2118/14.

Instructions regarding War Diaries and Intelligence Summaries are contained in F. S. Regs., Part II. and the Staff Manual respectively. Title pages will be prepared in manuscript.

WAR DIARY
or
INTELLIGENCE SUMMARY.
(Erase heading not required.)

Army Form C. 2118.

(11.)

Place	Date	Hour	Summary of Events and Information	Remarks and references to Appendices
IN THE LINE	21/9/17	(Contd.)	altered S.O.S. lines according to orders from D.M.G.O. At the time only twelve guns were available. The night was relatively quiet.	
"	22/9/17	–	Devoted the morning to cleaning up + readjustments. S.A.A. reserve changeover proved of great value in keeping guns in action. The morning was very quiet + the conditions remained good. Aerial activity + counter battery work throughout the day. Warned of probable relief next day. O.C. 123 Coy. arrived to arrange details of relief at 6.30 pm. The night was again quiet.	
"	23/9/17	–	S.O.S. signal at 4.30 am. This group was the first to answer it. Fired in decreasing intensity till 5.15 am. The morning was quiet. Four guns of right battery were relieved by four guns 123 Coy. at 9 am. Remaining guns were withdrawn in accordance with instructions. Relief complete at 10 am. There were three casualties during the relief. The Company was again in camp by 12 noon. Received orders at 1 pm to move to new area. Transport marched out at 5 pm, + personnel of sections followed by bus at 8 pm.	

Army Form C. 2118.

(12)

Instructions regarding War Diaries and Intelligence Summaries are contained in F. S. Regs., Part II. and the Staff Manual respectively. Title pages will be prepared in manuscript.

WAR DIARY
or
INTELLIGENCE SUMMARY.
(Erase heading not required.)

Place	Date	Hour	Summary of Events and Information	Remarks and references to Appendices
METEREN	23/9/17	(contd.)	Route via BAILLEUL + METEREN to farm at R32d. Comfortable quarters in barns + huts. Company settled by 11pm.	SHEET 27.
"	24/9/17	—	Paraded 10 am – 12.30 pm. + 2pm. – 4pm. to clean guns etc. Pay parade at 4/pm. Weather good + all ranks in excellent spirits. Officers conference at 11 am. to discuss operations + the lessons to be learned from them.	
"	25/9/17	—	Inspected the Company at 9am. All ranks seemed fit. Morning spent in further cleaning + reorganising. Lectures by section officers during afternoon dealing with lessons of the operations. Reorganised the company by making it into six sections instead of four with an establishment for each, all surplus being kept in reserve in Hq. Section to be posted as required. Made necessary promotions in N.C.O's. Lt. Manning reported for duty. The Company was congratulated by G.O.C. Bge. on its share in the recent operations.	
"	26/9/17	—	Tested new guns on range. Arranged baths for all ranks. Rendered reports on operations + the lessons learned from them. The Company was congratulated by G.O.C. Division on its share in the operations of the 19th – 23rd insts. 34 O.R. reported for duty as carriers. These are from the infantry	

A7092. Wt. W128.9/M1293. 750,000. 1/17. D.D & I. Ltd. Forms/C2118/14.

Army Form C. 2118.

(13)

WAR DIARY
or
INTELLIGENCE SUMMARY.
(Erase heading not required.)

Instructions regarding War Diaries and Intelligence Summaries are contained in F. S. Regs., Part II. and the Staff Manual respectively. Title pages will be prepared in manuscript.

Place	Date	Hour	Summary of Events and Information	Remarks and references to Appendices
METEREN	26/9/17	-	units in the Brigade. Weather conditions continued excellent.	
"	27/9/17	-	Inspections by Section officers. Inspected carriers & found them a mixed draft. Continued salvaging & reorganising. Made a redistribution of limbers, withdrew Barr & Stroud Rangefinders & Prismatic Binoculars to store. Football competition during afternoon & evening. Arranged for the Divisional Band to be present. Received orders at 10pm to move next day to new area. Issued preliminary orders accordingly.	
"	28/9/17	-	Spent the morning in preparation for move to new area. Paraded at noon & passed rendez-vous to time. Held up on road by congestion of infantry near BERTHEN. Marched via BERTHEN to CONQUEROR camp one mile N.W. of WESTOUTRE. Arrived 3pm. & went under canvas. Accomodation scarce but sufficient in the good weather conditions prevailing.	
CONQUEROR CAMP WESTOUTRE.	29/9/17	-	Paraded as follows — Section inspections, cleaning limbers & guns etc., gun & barrage drill. Afternoon devoted to fitting pack saddles in view of operations. Lt. Boswell returned from course at CAMIERS. 2 RAMC orderlies attached for operations as result of representations made after last action. Warned to move forward on following day.	

A7092. Wt. W12839/M1293. 750,000. 1/17. D. D & L. Ltd. Forms/C2118/14.

Instructions regarding War Diaries and Intelligence Summaries are contained in F. S. Regs., Part II. and the Staff Manual respectively. Title pages will be prepared in manuscript.

WAR DIARY
or
INTELLIGENCE SUMMARY.
(Erase heading not required.)

(14)

Army Form C. 2118.

Place	Date	Hour	Summary of Events and Information	Remarks and references to Appendices
WESTOUTRE to SCOTTISH WOOD	30/9/17.	–	Met D.M.G.O. by appointment at HALLEBAST CORNER at 7.45 am. Proceeded to line & selected battery positions in POLYGON WOOD. 110th Bde. took over from Australians. The enemy was very active throughout the area & conditions generally were difficult. Completed reconnaissance & returned to SCOTTISH WOOD where the company arrived at 4 pm. having route marched from WESTOUTRE. Under canvas for the night in SCOTTISH WOOD. O.C. companies conference at 3pm. at D.M.G.O's Hqs. to decide details re battery positions. Sent Lt. Boswell to line with party of Sappers attached for the operations from the Bde. R.E. Coy. He had instructions to proceed with the work of preparing the battery position, dugout accommodation, belt filling depots etc. Sent in 100,000 SAA. by limbers & pack mules as far as GLENCORSE WOOD. The enemy were very active throughout the night but the parties sent up suffered no casualties.	
			J. Chalmers Captain, Cmdg. 62nd M.G. Coy.	

A7092) Wt. W128.9/M1293. 750,000. 1/17. D. D & L. Ltd. Forms/C2118/14.

Appendise "A"

SECRET.

Copy No. 7.

62nd MACHINE GUN COMPANY.
Operation Order No.1/17.

Map Reference "ZILLEBEKE" 1/10,000. 17th Sept. 1917.

1. INTENTION. The 41st Division will take part in the forthcoming operations of the Xth Corps. It will attack on a front extending from J.19.b.55.10 to a point South of CROSS ROADS J.25.d.30.98. The following objectives will be attacked and captured:-

(a) RED LINE. J.20.a.80.00 to J.26.a.40.00.

(b) BLUE LINE. J.20.d.60.70 to J.26.d.10.95.

(c) GREEN LINE. J.21.c.90.80 to J.26.d.75.90.

2. DISTRIBUTION. The operations will be carried out on ATTACK DAY. The 39th Division will operate on the right and the 23rd Division on the left of the 41st Division. The 124th Inf. Bde. will be the right and the 122nd Inf. Bde. will be the left attacking Bde. The 123rd Inf. Bde. will be in Divisional Reserve. The 62nd Machine Gun Company will co-operate on the 41st Division frontage in conjunction with the 64th Machine Gun Company.

3. BOUNDARIES, etc. Divisional Boundaries, Dumps, Signal Stations, Dressing Stations and Headquarters have been notified verbally and pointed out onthe map.

4. ALLOCATION OF SECTIONS.
(1) The 62nd Machine Gun Company will form a group of two batteries. The group willbe commanded by the Company Commander, with Lt.TIPTAFT as 2nd i/command. Each battery will be composed of two Sections of fourguns each as follows:-

Right Battery (4C). Nos. 3 & 4 Sections.
Battery Commander - Lt.CLARKE.
Battery 2nd i/command - 2/Lt.TILLOTSON.

Left Battery (4D). Nos. 1 & 2 Sections.
Battery Commander -Lt.LESLIE.
Battery 2nd i/command - Lt.STEPHENSON.

(2) The right battery will belocated in the position prepared between J.25.a.35.60 and J.25.a.37.75.
The left battery will be located in the position prepared between J.25.a.35.80 and J.25.a.37.92.

5. MOVES. Batteries will move into position asfollows.
Dress - fighting order with greatcoats.
(1) 18th inst. Battery Commanders, Section Sergts, Gun Commanders, Nos.1 & 2 of each gun & signallers will embus at 5 p.m. and proceed to positions. They will devote the following day to checking lines and other final preparations.

(2) 19th inst. Battery 2nds i/command, Sub-Section Sergts, and Nos. 3 & 4 of each gun, and theartificer will embus at 5 p.m. and proceed to positions.

6. ACTION OF GROUP.
(1) Barrage Lines, S.O.S. Lines and all necessary data are published in the Fire Organisation Orders attached.

(2) S.O.S. Barrage. At ZERO plus 5 hrs.15 mins. the barrage will cease, but all batteries will be ready to answer the S.O.S. call by establishing a barrage along the final lines.

The success of the barrage depends on the promptitude with which it is put down. The S.O.S. is a rifle grenade signal parachute with three colours - Red over Green over Yellow. Any changes in this signal will be notified.

(3) Switches. All batteries will be prepared to concentrate their fire on any area where the enemy is resisting or concentrating for counter attack. Battery Commanders will receive orders for such switches from the Group Commander.

(4) Battery Commanders will detail one gun per battery to deal with low flying enemy aircraft. These guns will fire from reversed tripods. They will take part in the ordinary barrages but will be devoted to anti-aircraft work as necessary. Anti-aircraft sights for these guns can be drawn from Stores.

(5) Practice Barrages. The left battery will carry out practice barrages in accordance with instructions issued separately.

(6) Harassing Fire. The right battery will carry out harassing fire on the night preceding the attack, in accordance with instructions issued separately.

7. COMMUNICATIONS. Telephonic communication is provided between Group & Battery Headquarters. O.C. Left Battery will be responsible for detailing Signallers as follows:-

To Right Battery Headquarters. ..	2
Left Battery & Group Headquarters.	2
D.M.G.O. at 124th Inf. Bde. Headquarters, HEDGE ST. TUNNELS.	2 (by 6 p.m. on ATTACK DAY minus one).

He will ensure that all Signallers become thoroughly acquainted with all Headquarters and routes between them on the 19th inst.

8. SYNCHRONISATION OF WATCHES. Lieut. TIPTAFT will synchronise watches at D.M.G.O's Battle Headquarters, Nos. 1 & 2 LARK ROW, HEDGE ST. TUNNELS, on ATTACK DAY minus one at 6 p.m. Battery Commanders will synchronise at Group Headquarters at 7 p.m. on that day.

9. ATTACK DAY & ZERO HOUR. These will be notified later.

10. RATIONS & WATER. The party moving into position on the 18th inst. will carry 48 hours rations complete. The party moving up on the 19th inst. will carry 24 hours rations complete. Water for 19th & 20th inst. is at the battery positions.
Lt. DODSON will arrange for water & rations to be at CANADA TUNNELS on and after the 20th inst. at 7 p.m. nightly till further orders. Battery Commanders will arrange for parties to draw these.

11. S.A.A. An ample reserve is at battery positions.

12. REPAIRS. The armourer will be at Group Headquarters, and will visit guns as required.

13. TRANSPORT & DETAILS. These will remain in their present camp, Lt. DODSON being in charge.

14. FIRE DISCIPLINE. Attention is directed to the entries in the "Remarks" Column of "Fire Organisation Orders" and to Xth Corps appendix 3 issued herewith.

Capt.,
Comdg. 62 Coy. Machine Gun Corps.

Issued at 6 p.m.

DISTRIBUTION.

Copy No.	1	to	D.M.G.O., 41st Division.
" "	2	"	O.C., Company.
" "	3	"	File.
" "	4	"	Right Battery Commander.
" "	5	"	Left Battery Commander.
" "	6	"	O.i/c Details.
" "	7 & 8	"	War Diary.

Instructions regarding War Diaries and Intelligence Summaries are contained in F. S. Regs., Part II. and the Staff Manual respectively. Title pages will be prepared in manuscript.

WAR DIARY
or
INTELLIGENCE SUMMARY.
(Erase heading not required.)

Army Form C. 2118.

(1)

62nd M G Coy
Vol 20

Place	Date	Hour	Summary of Events and Information	Remarks and references to Appendices
SCOTTISH WOOD near DICKEBUSH	1/10/17	–	Moved camp a mile further up; all ranks in bivouacks. Reported to O.C. units & arranged for attaching mobile guns for operations in accordance with instructions. Arranged for guns to report to respective units two hours before they moved to assembly positions. Sent up Nos. 1 & 2 Sects. to form barrage battery as arranged & prepared for. They carried in belt boxes & water from pack mule dump; casualties 2 O.R. wounded & one mule killed. Enemy very active during the night, work of carrying in hindered accordingly. Lt. Bagott reported for duty after one month's leave in U.K.	
"	2/10/17	–	Received operation orders from D.M.G.O. & Bde. & issued Coy. Op. Order. Officers conference at 10 am. Explained scheme in detail & gave instructions to particular officers i/c. mobile guns. Officers instructed N.C.Os. & completed preparations. No. IV Sect. paraded at 2 pm. & proceeded to join the Queen's. Guns etc. taken on pack mules. 4 carriers per team allotted from attached infantry. Pack mules took stores as far as possible when carrying was completed to assembly position by hand. 2nd/command made reconnaissance of line & reported the battery escaping shelling. Back areas heavily shelled. Two guns from No. III Sect. proceeded to join N.Fs & two to join Yorks. All teams 1 gun commander & 8 O.R. strong (including carriers). Pack mules	Appendix "A".

A7092 Wt. W128 9/M1293 750,000. 1/17. D. D & L. Ltd. Forms/C2118/14.

Army Form C. 2118.

(2)

WAR DIARY
or
INTELLIGENCE SUMMARY.

(Erase heading not required.)

Instructions regarding War Diaries and Intelligence Summaries are contained in F. S. Regs., Part II. and the Staff Manual respectively. Title pages will be prepared in manuscript.

Place	Date	Hour	Summary of Events and Information	Remarks and references to Appendices
			used as far as possible. Settled details with D.M.G.O. & Staff Captain at Divisional Hq. Lt. Tillotson wounded; 1 O.R. killed & 4 wounded.	
Coy. Hq. in the line.	3/10/17	–	Proceeded to adv. Hq. at 12 noon. Arrived 2pm. & made arrangements to connect with Bge. by 'phone. Visited battery at 3.30pm. & found everything ready. Sent Lt. Manning to replace 2/Lt. Tillotson (wounded) with detachments attached Queen's. Visited O.C. Group & made necessary arrangements with him re barrage. Battery now under his command except for administration. Returned & reported to D.M.G.O. at adv. Hq. at CHATEAU WOOD. Enemy shelled back areas heavily but conditions otherwise good. He used gas shells at intervals throughout the night. Experienced great difficulty in keeping up telephone wires owing to shelling. Reported at Bge. Hq. at 2am. & succeeded in reestablishing communication. Enemy shelling freely at 5am.	
"	4/10/17	–	Zero at 6am. Conditions were very favourable. By 7.15am. first prisoners were down at Bge. Hq. First objectives definitely reported captured & consolidated at 8.30am. Enemy shelling which had been heavy on back areas now lifted & concentrated forward. Battery carried out barrages as laid down. Detachment to 1st objective reached its positions & dug in. 2/Lt. Manning wounded. Section with right	

A7092 Wt. W125 9/M1293 750,000. 1/17. D. D & L. Ltd. Forms/C2118/14.

Instructions regarding War Diaries and Intelligence Summaries are contained in F. S. Regs., Part II. and the Staff Manual respectively. Title pages will be prepared in manuscript.

WAR DIARY
or
INTELLIGENCE SUMMARY.
(Erase heading not required.)

Army Form C. 2118.

Place	Date	Hour	Summary of Events and Information	Remarks and references to Appendices
			Battn. (N.F.s) got through without casualties until getting in front of 64th Bge on their right they came under enemy enfilade fire & suffered their casualties. Getting into position they got excellent direct fire on the enemy to the South using a captured gun in addition to their own. They continued in this position three days doing excellent work. Detachment with left Battn. (YORKS & subsequently LINCS) lost direction & found themselves in 7th Div. area. Lt. Dodson was wounded. Battery completed barrages as laid down & stood by on S.O.S. lines: See report appended.	Appendix "B"
			General situation meantime obscure as 5th Div. on right was held up so that 64 Bge was forming a defensive flank. 7 Div. on left got all objectives as did left Battn. of this Bge. Remained with D.M.G.O. at his Hq. during the day. On hearing news of casualties of C.O.s 64 & 237 Coys. I was sent up to take over command of the Groups in POLYGON WOOD & to arrange the M.G. defense of the captured ground. Took over command at midnight.	
POLYGON WOOD.	5/10/17	–	Situation quiet throughout the night. Made reconnaissance of forward area between two & three a.m. & located Hqs. of Battns. Went out again at 9 a.m. & found guns in first objective & continued throughout the area with a view to M.G. defense. Reorganised Groups during the day. New S.O.S. lines laid down.	

A7092 W. W125.9/M1293. 750,000. 1/17. D. D & L. Ltd. Forms/C2118/14.

Army Form C. 2118.

Instructions regarding War Diaries and Intelligence Summaries are contained in F. S. Regs., Part II. and the Staff Manual respectively. Title pages will be prepared in manuscript.

WAR DIARY
or
INTELLIGENCE SUMMARY.

(Erase heading not required.)

(4.)

Place	Date	Hour	Summary of Events and Information	Remarks and references to Appendices
			Enemy ranging throughout the day. His M.G. fire from the South enfilading our area. Conditions normal. Three guns in the battery + one in the first objective had been knocked out. Many of the carriers were reported missing. M.G. personnel in excellent spirits especially in forward sections.	
POLYGON WOOD.	6/10/17	–	Made further reconnaissance & moved four guns from 1st objective to new positions with a view to the situation on the South. Situation less quiet. Enemy sniping & M.G. fire was marked throughout the day. Weather broken. Good shooting still obtained by night detachment in REUTEL. Barrage battery was not called on. Got rations, water & ammn. up to battery position on pack mules. Transport did excellent work. (vide Report.)	Appendix "B"
"	7/10/17	–	Normal conditions throughout the day. Made arrangements for relief by 110th Coy. Relief began at 11pm. under fairly good conditions. Line of approach (CLAPHAM JUNCTN., GLENCORSE WOOD, & BLACK WATCH CORNER) under continual shell fire, was accountable for a high percentage of the casualties suffered. Forward area more quiet so that relief forward of battery was	

A7092 Wt. W128 9/M1293 750,000. 1/17. D. D & L. Ltd. Forms/C2118/14.

Instructions regarding War Diaries and Intelligence Summaries are contained in F. S. Regs., Part II. and the Staff Manual respectively. Title pages will be prepared in manuscript.

WAR DIARY
or
INTELLIGENCE SUMMARY.
(Erase heading not required.)

Army Form C. 2118.

(31)

Place	Date	Hour	Summary of Events and Information	Remarks and references to Appendices
			without incident.	
CAMP (SCOTTISH WOOD)	8/10/17	-	Company complete in camp by 10am. Received warning order we move on following day.	
	9/10/17	-	Morning spent in packing limbers. Transport moved at 1pm. en route for rest area by road, halting for the night at CAESTRE. Company paraded at 3pm. & marched to OUDERDOM. Entrained at 4.30pm. & detrained at EBHINGHAM at 1 am. on the 10th inst.	
WALLON CAPELLE.	10/10/17	-	Marched to billets near WALLON CAPELLE arriving 3am. Transport arrived at 11am. Spent the day in settling down in new billets. Accommodation excellent though scattered.	
	11/10/17	-	Devoted the day to cleaning equipment & gun stores. Hindered by weather which was wet & cold. Equipment (gun) had been greatly depleted by handing over to 110th Coy. on relief. Men were not in good spirits & little progress was made.	
	12/10/17	-	Weather improved. Continued cleaning & made better progress. A draft of 37 O.R. arrived. Carriers from infantry continued with the Coy. in view of probable operations.	

A7092 Wt. W128.9/M1293 750,000. 1/17. D. D & L. Ltd. Forms/C2118/14.

Instructions regarding War Diaries and Intelligence Summaries are contained in F. S. Regs., Part II. and the Staff Manual respectively. Title pages will be prepared in manuscript.

WAR DIARY
or
INTELLIGENCE SUMMARY.
(Erase heading not required.)

Army Form C. 2118.

(6)

Place	Date	Hour	Summary of Events and Information	Remarks and references to Appendices
WALLON CAPELLE.	13/10/17	-	Section inspections, gun drill & T.O.E.T. occupied the morning. Inspected draft & found it good in personnel but with comparatively little training the average being 5 weeks. The afternoon was devoted to recreation.	
	14/10/17	-	C.O's Inspection. The parade was very good on the whole except for the transport Section & the attached infantry. Men were looking more fit & apparently were recovering. Football occupied the afternoon & a concert the evening.	
	15/10/17	-	C.O's Inspection of Transport. Poor turn out partly accounted for by the wet weather. Barrage drill practised by sections. Started revolver competition in the afternoon - No.1 Sect. v No.2 Sect. S.M's class for junior N.C.O's began; instruction in duties of various ranks.	
	16/10/17	-	Section Inspections followed by general training including Company Drill & Barrage Drill by half companies. Revolver competition during afternoon - No.3 Sect. v No.4 Sect. S.M. class continued. Weather good & all ranks in better spirits.	
	17/10/17	-	Parades as for 16th inst.	

A7092 Wt. W12S.9/M1293 750,000. 1/17. D. D & L. Ltd. Forms/C2118/14.

Instructions regarding War Diaries and Intelligence Summaries are contained in F. S. Regs., Part II. and the Staff Manual respectively. Title pages will be prepared in manuscript.

WAR DIARY
or
INTELLIGENCE SUMMARY.
(Erase heading not required.)

Army Form C. 2118.

(7)

Place	Date	Hour	Summary of Events and Information	Remarks and references to Appendices
	18/10/17	-	Parades as above: Weather excellent. Held a boxing competition during the afternoon which was very popular.	
	19/10/17	-	Prepared to move in accordance with instructions received.	
DICKEBUSH	20/10/17	-	Transport marched out at 1pm. & the Coy. at 4.30pm. Transport bivouacked for the night at EECKE. Coy. entrained at EBLINGHAM at 7pm. & detrained at DICKEBUSH at 1.30am. attached to camp near HALLEBAST CORNER (MICMAC CAMP). All ranks under canvas.	
	21/10/17	-	Transport arrived at 11am. Went to COY. H.Q. 68th M.G. Coy. in the line with D.M.G.O. & arranged reliefs. All approaches were heavily shelled by the enemy. 68th Coy. had ten guns in the line. Returned to camp at 7pm. & issued orders for relief.	
IN THE LINE (E of POLYGON WOOD)	22/10/17	-	Four teams left camp at 4.30am. taking guns, spare parts, rations & water. Arrived HELLFIRE CORNER at 6.30am. where traffic was blocked. Left limbers here & marched to HOOGE CRATER. ~~Limbers were late.~~ Set out again at 8am. & relieved without casualties. Relief complete by 11am. Conditions were quiet on this sector but ~~there~~ was great artillery activity to N. & S. Visited four guns	

A7092. Wt. W125 9/M1293. 750,000. 1/17. D. D & L. Ltd. Forms/C2118/14.

Instructions regarding War Diaries and Intelligence Summaries are contained in F. S. Regs., Part II. and the Staff Manual respectively. Title pages will be prepared in manuscript.

WAR DIARY
or
INTELLIGENCE SUMMARY.
(Erase heading not required.)

Army Form C. 2118.

Place	Date	Hour	Summary of Events and Information	Remarks and references to Appendices
	22/10/17	-	during the afternoon. Teams collected S.A.A. and timber during the evening. Visited front line guns between 4.30 pm. + 6 pm. Found left gun well sited but right gun with no field of fire. Altered accordingly. Conditions quiet except for sniping. Shelling began at dusk but night was relatively quiet. All except front line teams were in "meluses" with good accomodation.	
	23/10/17	-	2/Lt. Goddart with two teams reported at 6.30 am. + took over two positions from 64th Coy. in accordance with D.M.G.O. instructions. Limbers with rations + SAA did not get up to Coy. Hq. as intended owing to bad state of country. Had to carry by hand accordingly. Visited guns at NOORDEMDHOEK. Sited all positions + fields of fire. Visited S.O.S. guns which were now well dug in + had got up 36,000 SAA. in view of proposed barrage scheme in connection with forthcoming operations. Exchanged COY. Hqs. with O.C. 64th Coy. Conditions bad owing to intermittent rain throughout the day. Continued work on all positions. Only consistent activity by the enemy was a barrage on front line at 11 am. + the	

Instructions regarding War Diaries and Intelligence Summaries are contained in F. S. Regs., Part II. and the Staff Manual respectively. Title pages will be prepared in manuscript.

WAR DIARY
or
INTELLIGENCE SUMMARY.
(Erase heading not required.)

Army Form C. 2118.

(9.)

Place	Date	Hour	Summary of Events and Information	Remarks and references to Appendices
			steady shelling of approaches. One gun was put out of action by shell fire.	
	24/10/17	-	Relieved front line teams by 2 teams from reserve under Lt. Goddard. Withdrew relieved teams to Coy. H.Q. There were therefore now 14 guns in the line. Orders for barrages for forthcoming operations received from D.M.G.O. Worked out calculations. Day spent in getting up ammn. for the barrage. Situation normal but weather very wet & ground in very bad state. Got up two days rations & water & 30,000 SAA.	
	25/10/17	-	Further 20,000 SAA brought up together with all material required for barrage. New barrage lines advised from D.M.G.O. Altered accordingly. Laid out new lines & completed emplacements. All preparations complete by 4 p.m. Visited all barrage positions. Weather cold with strong wind making very favourable conditions for attack.	
	26/10/17	-	Zero at 5.40 am. M.Gs. opened at Z + 3 mins. according to programme. Two casualties in first few minutes & gun put out by direct hit. Remainder fired well & were untouched throughout the action. 1 belt per 4 mins till Z + 20 mins. & 1 belt per 8 min. from	

A7092 Wt. W128 9/M1293 750,000. 1/17. D. D & L Ltd. Forms/C2118/14.

WAR DIARY
or
INTELLIGENCE SUMMARY.
(Erase heading not required.)

Army Form C. 2118.

(10)

Instructions regarding War Diaries and Intelligence Summaries are contained in F. S. Regs., Part II. and the Staff Manual respectively. Title pages will be prepared in manuscript.

Place	Date	Hour	Summary of Events and Information	Remarks and references to Appendices
			Z+20' to Z+120' when all guns ceased fire & laid on S.O.S. lines. There was little enemy retaliation on our sector. Remainder of day was quiet. Visited front line guns during afternoon. Conditions in trenches very bad owing to weather & shelling. Relieved these front teams by this from barrage positions.	
	27/10/17	-	A quiet day. The attack on the south had failed but on the north had succeeded. Activity seemed to be on these fronts. Weather & general conditions better. Had three A.A. mountings sent up & fixed in positions at S.O.S. emplacements. O.C. 110th Coy. came up to arrange relief. Fixed details with him for 29th inst.	
	28/10/17	-	D.M.G.O. visited guns. Various changes decided upon; all guns to be sited taking cover from mebuses & either firing over the tops of these or round the sides. Worked on these accordingly. Conditions exceptionally quiet. Visited front line guns during the afternoon, & moved a third gun into front line to cover left batt. frontage.	
	29/10/17	-	Relieved by 110th Coy., first teams arriving at 8 am. Relief without incident & complete by 10 am. Company concentration camp at	

Instructions regarding War Diaries and Intelligence Summaries are contained in F. S. Regs., Part II. and the Staff Manual respectively. Title pages will be prepared in manuscript.

WAR DIARY
or
INTELLIGENCE SUMMARY.

(Erase heading not required.)

Army Form C. 2118.

(11)

Place	Date	Hour	Summary of Events and Information	Remarks and references to Appendices
			SCOTTISH WOOD by noon. Under canvas. Good accomodation but ground very muddy.	
SCOTTISH WOOD. (ANZAC CAMP)	30/10/17	-	Parades for cleaning guns stores equipment. Weather wet. Camp fatigues throughout the day. Office work. Deficiencies rendered.	
	31/10/17	-	Three sections at training & one on camp fatigues. Filled belts & overhauled ammn. etc. Pay parade at 2pm.	

J.W. Chalmers Capt.
Cmdg.
124 M.G.C.

62 Machine Gun Coy.

Report on Operations in connection with the attack on 4th October 1917.
MAP REFERENCE - GHELUVELT, 1/10,000.

A. BARRAGE BATTERY.

No. 2 Barrage Group was originally composed of one battery of eight guns from each of 62 & 64 Companies. Positions were sited at J.10.c.00.20 on the 30th Sept., 62 Coy. being the Right (C) Battery. A mebus was selected as Battery H.Q., and the Battery Commander moved in that night, taking with him his Section Sergt and the 5 Sappers attached from the 97th R.E.Coy. for the operations. His orders were to reclaim as much dugout accommodation as possible for his battery, prepare barrage gun positions and store S.A.A. Concurrently the Sub-Battery Commander was detailed to superintend the ammunition supply. 100,000 S.A.A. was conveyed by limbers as far as the W. edge of GLENCORSE WOOD, and thence by packmules to a point 100 yds. W. of BLACK WATCH CORNER. From this point the ammunition was carried by hand to the battery position where it was cached under supervision of the Battery Commander. Water, belt boxes and tripods were dealt with in the same way. This work occupied two nights, so that on the evening of the 2nd/3rd the personnel of the battery moved into position, taking with them the actual guns, spare parts, aiming posts, spare barrels and oil. The principle adopted throughout was that the junior Officer dealt with everything as far as the battery position, while the senior Officer made all the arrangements at the position itself. This answered admirably. By the afternoon of the 3rd inst. the battery was ready for action. At 2 p.m. on that date the command of the Battery passed to Group 2 Commander (O.C. 64 Coy.) This Officer supplied all fighting charts, fire organisation orders etc., from which the battery commander issued his gun orders, the battery being now only under my command for supplies.

On going in on the 2nd, rations for two days were carried, so that it was not necessary to send up until the afternoon of the 4th. The attack having been successful I decided to carry out the plans originally made, namely to take a pack train right up to the battery position by daylight. This was successfully accomplished on the 4th and following days. By this use of mules much fatigue was saved, and the whole difficulty of ration parties getting lost at night was overcome. During the whole week of operations, only five mules became casualties; the supply of rations, water, ammunition etc. was guaranteed, and this was accomplished on that notoriously bad line of approach through GLENCORSE WOOD and BLACK WATCH CORNER.

At 12 midnight on the night of the 4th/5th October, I took over command of Group 2 in succession to O.C., 64 Coy. wounded. In accordance with instructions from D.M.G.O., I at once altered the S.O.S. lines and reorganised the Group, several guns having been put out of action, and many casualties having occurred in the personnel. An S.O.S. was answered at dawn, fire being sustained for thirty minutes. The confidence with which the gun numbers answered the S.O.S. was noticeable, all guns opening out automatically on the signal going up. Several hours belt filling followed, but from this point these batteries ceased to take an active part in the operations. They were not again called on for S.O.S. or for concentrations, and consequently stood by until relieved on the night of the 7th/8th inst. For five days therefore "C" Battery remained in action. In this time it had four guns destroyed, and suffered 14 casualties. It carried out its duties under the most trying conditions, its ability to do so being in a great measure dependent on the excellent work of the Company's transport. As an example of what can be done by an M.G. battery, this case cannot compare with the action of the 20th September, but here the

/conditions

conditions were infinitely worse. The time and preparations necessary to successful battery work were not possible, but even so a result was obtained which did much towards the success of the operations.

B. MOBILE GUNS.
Eight guns of this unit were detailed as mobile guns, to accompany the 62nd Infantry Brigade. Four were sent to consolidate each objective. The distribution was therefore;

To 3/4th The Queens (RWS) Regt.	4.
12/13th Northumberland Fusilrs.	2.
10th Yorkshire Regt.	2.

Each detachment was sent to the unit with which it was detailed to operate and joined it in each case on the day it proceeded to assembly positions in the line. 4 Infantry carriers from the attached strength were attached to each team, making a total strength of 1 Gun Commander and 8 O.R. per gun. With this personnel each team went into action with 4 Gallons of water and 15 belt-boxes. The whole outfit of each detachment was loaded on pack mules and proceeded as far as possible by this means. Difficulties began from the point at which mules were unloaded. The broken nature of the ground and the varying speed of the Infantry movements caused great difficulty in keeping in touch. Two detachments reached their assembly places. The third i.e. the two guns attached to the 10th Yorks.Regt. got out of touch and found themselves still out of communication with their Infantry at ZERO hour. Further difficulties arose owing to casualties to Officers. All three were wounded though one (with North Fus) remained at duty. I sent another Officer to take command of the 4 gun detachment with the 3/4th The Queens (RWS) Regt. and he too was wounded shortly after ZERO, thus leaving only one Officer in action out of four who went up. With the Officers gone, the usual difficulty in keeping carriers together was experienced. Adding to this the occurrence of casualties, only eight boxes on an average arrived in the final positions with each gun.
The four guns detailed for the first objective reached it and got into position under the command of the Section Sergt. The value of Officers going over in detail with their N.C.Os. all that is to be done was well exemplified. Had this not been done the N.C.O. in question could not have carried on as he did. While not getting his guns just where they were intended to be, he nevertheless, carried out the plan laid down, so that when I reached him on the morning of the 5th inst. he had a pair of guns on the right flank of the first objective and one covering the left. The fourth gun had been destroyed during the advance.
The final position having been consolidated by the 4th, I redistributed these guns, pushing two further out to the right flank to a more commanding position, and bringing two back to the spur behind in order to increase the volume of fire on the valley to the South.
Advancing with the North.Fus. a detachment of two guns had pushed forward to the final objective, but had ultimately lost direction and found themselves in front of the Infantry of 64 Bde. The position however, was excellent, both offensively and defensively and the Officer in charge decided to retain it. He obtained most effective observation and consequently had direct shooting on the enemy. Keeping a necessary reserve on hand for defensive purposes he fired all the ammunition he could collect. Unfortunately, owing to casualties to eight successive runners, he was out of touch with me for two days. Owing to his isolated position in front of 64 Bde. I did not succeed in locating him during my reconnaissance on the 5th inst. He held on however, and both guns came through untouched, having been in action for three days. These were undoubtedly most efficient guns.
The detachment on the left with the 10th Yorks.Regt. did not get sufficiently far forward during the attack. The Officer was wounded in the early stages, but in this instance, the sergeant

did not succeed in getting the guns to the required point. He lost direction and got into the 7th Division area, getting up well to the left of the 62nd Bde. These guns consequently had no offensive value, and were not called upon for defence. The total casualties in the personnel of thC mobile guns totals 25. Throughout the operations there was a marked absence of low-flying enemy aeroplanes, so that no A.A. fire was carried out. Of the attached personnel, I wish to bring to notice the valuable work of the two R.A. .C. orderlies. They rendered a great service to my company and were in every way an entire success.
The Sappers too, did excellent work. They were severely handicapped by the counter-attack on the morning of the 1st Oct. when for the time being they became infantry, but despite adverse circumstances, they did valuable work.
The carriers were of mixed quality. Some stuck to their work and did very well indeed: others caused much trouble. A larger proportion of N.C.Os. would have made a great difference. Two junior lance-corporals were totally incapable of dealing with their thirty-two men, and I could not spare my own N.C.Os. from their own duties. A full N.C.O. from each Battalion would have increased the value of these carriers 100%.

12/10/1917.

J. W. Chalmers Capt. Commanding,
62nd Coy. Machine Gun Corps.

SECRET. Copy No. 14

62nd Coy. Machine Gun Corps.

Map Refs.

GHELUVELT. 1/10,000
All sheets issued showing POLYGON WOOD.

1. Intention. The 2nd Army will attack on a day to be notified later.
The Xth Corps will co-operate in this attack with the object of establishing our front line on the remaining high ground in the possession of the enemy.

2. Distribution. The operations will be carried out by the 5th Division on the Right, and the 7th Division on the Left of the 21st Division. The attack and capture of the 1st objective will be carried out by the 3/4th The Queens (RWS) Regt. The attack and capture of the 2nd objective will be carried out by the 12/13th N.Fs. on the Right and the 10th Yorks.Regt. om the Left. The 1st Lincoln Regt. will be in Brigade reserve. The 62nd M.G.Coy. will co-operate.

3. Boundaries. Divisional and Brigade Boundaries, Objectives, Dumps, Dressing Stations, and Headquarters have been notified verbally, and pointed out ontthe map.

4. Allocation of Sections. The Company will be organised as two half-companies. (a) Nos.1 & 2 Sections will form a barrage a battery, Nos. 3 & 4 Sections will form mobile detachments to accompany the infantry in the attack.
(a) Barrage Battery.
This battery will be commanded by Lieut. J BOSWELL with 2/Lieut. MANNING as 2nd/i/command. It will form part of No.2 Group and will be lettered "C" battery. Battery Hqrs. will be at J 9c 9/1. The battery commander under ~~Hxxx~~. instructions previously issued will make all necessary preparations for the accomodation of personnel and material and will prepare battery positions. All preparations must be completed by noon on the 3rd inst. The Battery commander will be directly under the orders of No.2 Group commander (Capt.DIXON) from the time of this Officer's arrival at Group Hqrs until further orders.
(b) Mobile Detachments.
(1) No.4 Section under 2/Lieut. TILLOTSON will be attached to the 3/4th The Queens (RWS) Regt. from 3 p.m. on the 2nd inst. until further orders. O.C. No.4 Section will proceed to join this battalion under orders issued separately. This Section will work in two detachments of 2 guns each these being disposed on either flank of the attacking frontage of the battalion. After the consolidation of the first objective, these detachments are liable to be called upon to supplement the detachments going forward with the other two attacking battalions. All orders for such supplementing will come through the battalion commanders concerned. No.4 Section in turn will draw upon the reserve at battery h rs. Reference to para. 7 will show detail of supply.
(2) No.3 Section. This Section will be divided into two detachments as follows:-
(a) Two teams under Lieut. DODSON will report to O.C. 10th Yorks.Regt. at 3 p.m. on the 3rd inst. and will be attached to this battalion until further orders. This detachment will move under orders issued separately.

It will be at the disposal of the O.C. 10th Yorks Regt. and will probab probably be employed on the extreme left flank of that unit. Its final position will be in the vicinity of J 11b 90/80.
Its night lines will be:-
Right Gun - Valley in J 6c & d.
Left Gun - Enfilade contour line 57 in J 12a.
By day it will engage all visible targets.
(b) Two teams under Lieut. CLARKE will report to O.C. 12/13th Northd.Fus. at 6 p.m. on the 2nd inst. and will be attached to this battalion until further orders. This detachment will move under orders issued separately. It will be at the disposal of O.C. 12/13th N.Fs. and will probably be employed on the Right flank of that unit. Its final position will be in the vicinity of J 11d 60/90. Its night lines will be:-
Right Gun - Enfilade Contour line 57 in J 12a.
Left Gun - Valley in J 12c.
By day it will engage all visible targets.

5. Attack Day and Zero Hour. These will be notified later.
S.O.S. The S.O.S. is by parachute rocket - RED over GREEN over YELLOW

6. Communications and Reports.
Mobile detachments will use their carriers as runners. All reports from the forward guns will be sent to Lieut. BOSWELL at battery Hqrs. He will forward all necessary correspondence to O.C Coy. at 62 Inf Bde Hqrs. J 13c 65/10. or to such other centre as may be ordered. The importance of detailed reports is emphasised. Immediately on taking up position Os C. mobile guns will send two runners each to battery headqrs. where they will be at the disposal of O.C battery for forwarding messages from C.O. to forward guns. The battery cable will always ~~will~~ be available for the forwarding of urgent messages through the battery commander.

7. Supply. S.A.A. water and rations will be available at battery hqrs. on and after the coming of "Attack Day". A pack train will deliver them to 2/Lieut MANNING who will issue on demand to ration parties from forward guns. Carriers from the first objective will take up all stores for their own and the front line teams to No.4 Sections positions. Front line detachments will draw from them accordingly.

8. Repairs. The Armourer will be at battery hqrs.

9. Medical. One R.A.M.C. orderly will be at battery hqrs. and one will accompany No.4 Section.

10. Administration. Coy.Orderly Room and Transport will remain in the present camp. The 2nd/i/command will be responsible that rations and water are delivered nightly on and after the 4th inst. at battery hqrs. and that S.A.A. replacements etc., are delivered there as required.

[signature] Capt.,
Commdg. 62nd Coy. M G Coy.,

Issued at 3 p.m.

Copy No.1. Bde Major. 62 Inf Bde.
2. D.M.G.O.
3. O.C. 3/4th The Queens (RWS) Regt.,
4. " 12/13th Northumberland Fus.
5. " 10th Yorkshire Regt.,
6. " Company.
7. " No.2 Group.
8. " "C" Battery.
9. " No.4 Section.
10. " Detachment with Northd. Fus.
11. " do. Yorks.Regt.
12. File.
13 & 14. War Diary.

Instructions regarding War Diaries and Intelligence Summaries are contained in F. S. Regs., Part II. and the Staff Manual respectively. Title pages will be prepared in manuscript.

WAR DIARY
or
~~INTELLIGENCE SUMMARY.~~ 62nd Heavy M.G. Corps

(Erase heading not required.)

Army Form C. 2118.

Vol 21

Place	Date	Hour	Summary of Events and Information	Remarks and references to Appendices
ANZAC CAMP. DICKEBUSH AREA.	1/11/17	-	Weather cold & wet; camp very muddy. Day spent in section training & camp fatigues. Enemy bombed vicinity of camp at night.	
"	2/11/17	-	Conditions same as for 1st inst. Lt. Biggott proceeded to U.K. for 6 months home service. Lt. Brassell took over duties of 2/command. 2/Lt. Knott reported for duty.	
"	3/11/17	-	General training & improvement of camp continued. Warning order to proceed to the line received, together with details of scheme for the 6th inst. Worked out necessary calculations & issued Op. Order re relief. Lt. Stephenson rejoined from leave; 1 O.R. (Transport Sergt.) reported for duty from A.H.T.D. Sent 40,000 S.A.A. to the line by pack train: 1 driver wounded (died of wounds), 1 mule killed & 2 wounded. Casualties occurred on MENIN RD.	APPENDIX "A".
"	4/11/17	-	Lt. Brassell appointed 2nd/command vice Lt. Biggott. Lt. Clarke proceeded on leave to U.K., 2/Lt. Kelsland taking over the duties of O/c. transport. Belt filling, inspection of First Dressings & preparation of guns etc. for the line occupied the day. Conditions improved.	
"	5/11/17	-	Coy. paraded at 4.15am. in accordance with Op. Order. Sent Coy. in limbers as far as HELL FIRE CORNER, from which point sections proceeded independently to the BUTTE de POLYGON where guides were waiting them. Relief of 110th Coy. complete at 9.15am. The morning was very	

A7092) Wt. W128/9/M1293. 750,000. 1/17. D. D & L. Ltd. Forms/C2118/14.

Instructions regarding War Diaries and Intelligence Summaries are contained in F. S. Regs., Part II. and the Staff Manual respectively. Title pages will be prepared in manuscript.

WAR DIARY
or
INTELLIGENCE SUMMARY.

(Erase heading not required.)

Army Form C. 2118.

(2)

Place	Date	Hour	Summary of Events and Information	Remarks and references to Appendices
ANZAC CAMP + In the Line			quiet & the Coy. got in without a casualty. C.O. made reconnaissance with O/C. Transport to find route via ZONNEBEEK with a view to taking mules through to Coy. Hq. Found road good except for a stretch of 300 yds. which was impassable for mules. Visited all barrage guns between 10am. & 1pm. & organised work on positions. Visited guns at NOORDEMDHOEK at 2pm. & settled details of work with Section Officer. Issued fire orders for front line guns. Situation generally was very quiet except for usual shelling of back areas. Aircraft was active. Section officers laid out lines for next day's shoot during the afternoon. The night was lively the enemy keeping up continuous shelling. Infantry carrying party of 15 O.R. reported for duty.	
In the Line	6/11/17	-	ZERO at 6am. M.Gs. opened at Z + 3 mins. according to orders. All guns fired well, & there were no casualties. Weather conditions during the morning were good but rain came on at 8.30 am. Enemy had the flanks of the attack located by 7am. & concentrated his artillery accordingly. He put down a very heavy & deep barrage on POLDERHOEK area. Guns remained on barrage lines till Z + 12 hrs when they changed to normal S.O.S. Our aircraft very active till 2pm. fifty two being counted in the air at once. Spasmodic shelling throughout the day. Went round front line guns during the afternoon. 1 O.R. wounded. Enemy sent over gas shells during the evening. Night quiet. One	

A7092) Wt. W128.9/M1293. 750,000. 1/17. D. D & L. Ltd. Forms/C2118/14.

Instructions regarding War Diaries and Intelligence Summaries are contained in F. S. Regs., Part II. and the Staff Manual respectively. Title pages will be prepared in manuscript.

WAR DIARY
or
INTELLIGENCE SUMMARY.
(Erase heading not required.)

(3)

Army Form C. 2118.

Place	Date	Hour	Summary of Events and Information	Remarks and references to Appendices
In the line		-	gun was damaged. Lt. Clarke awarded M.C. & C.S.M. Gazetted the D.C.M. 1 O.R. to M.G. School, Camiers.	
"	7/11/17	-	Army barrage at 5.30 am. Visited S.O.S. guns during the morning & arranged work. Rain had fallen overnight & conditions were bad. Visited positions. Work continued on all positions. Harassing fire was carried out on enemy lines of approach. Enemy patrol approached L3 position & was driven off by the team with bombs. Relieved all front line guns. 9 O.R. reported from Base for duty.	
"	8/11/17	-	Night quiet except for occasional gas shelling. Visited barrage guns & found work progressing well. Completed S.A.A. to 4,000 per gun, & belt boxes to 12 per gun. Got supply of sandbags forward & continued work on all emplacements. Enemy aircraft & M.Gs. active. 2 O.R. wounded. Carried out harassing fire & engaged aeroplanes. Enemy patrol again approached L3 position but was scattered by a burst of fire. Enemy aeroplane landed front line. Visited front line guns during the afternoon: Work on front line had greatly improved conditions. Night quiet but wet. 2/Lt. inspected Transport.	
"	9/11/17	-	Relieved all front line guns. Weather conditions very bad. Enemy	

A7092. Wt. W12839/M1293 750,000. 1/17. D. D & I. Ltd. Forms/C2118/14.

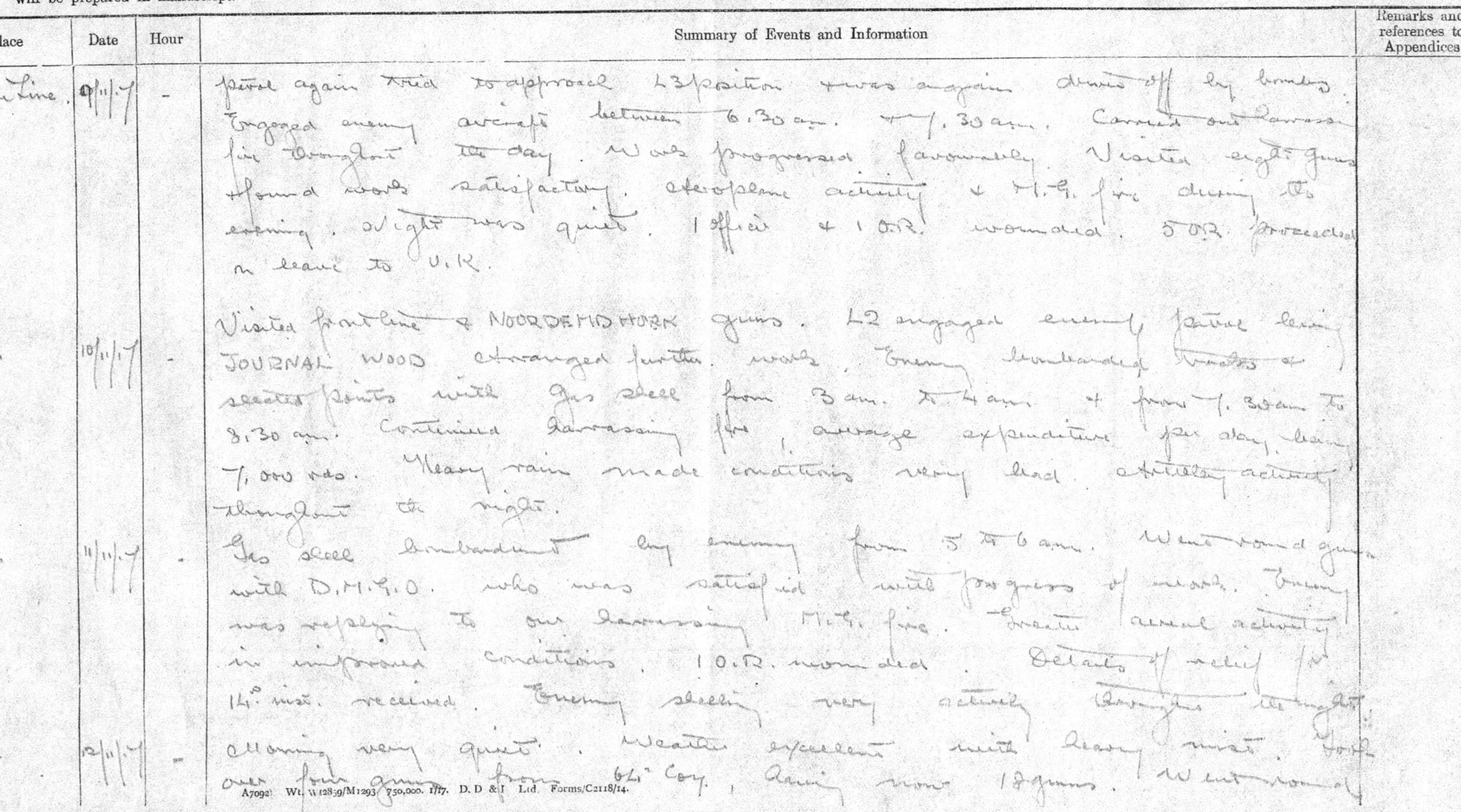

Instructions regarding War Diaries and Intelligence Summaries are contained in F. S. Regs., Part II. and the Staff Manual respectively. Title pages will be prepared in manuscript.

WAR DIARY
or
INTELLIGENCE SUMMARY.
(Erase heading not required.)

Army Form C. 2118.

(4)

Place	Date	Hour	Summary of Events and Information	Remarks and references to Appendices
In the Line.	9/11/17	-	Patrol again tried to approach L3 position & was again driven off by bombs. Engaged enemy aircraft between 6.30 am. & 7.30 am. Carried out harass fire throughout the day. Work progressed favourably. Visited eight guns & found work satisfactory. Aeroplane activity & M.G. fire during the evening. Night was quiet. 1 officer & 1 O.R. wounded. 5 O.R. proceeded on leave to U.K.	
"	10/11/17	-	Visited front line & NOORDEMDHOEK guns. L2 engaged enemy patrol leaving JOURNAL WOOD. Arranged further work. Enemy bombarded tracks & selected points with Gas shell from 3 am. to 4 am. & from 7.30 am to 8.30 am. Continued harassing fire, average expenditure per day being 7,000 rds. Heavy rain made conditions very bad. Artillery activity throughout the night.	
"	11/11/17	-	Gas shell bombardment by enemy from 5 to 6 am. Went round guns with D.M.G.O. who was satisfied with progress of work. Enemy was replying to our harassing M.G. fire. Greater aerial activity in improved conditions. 1 O.R. wounded. Details of relief for 14th inst. received. Enemy shelling very active throughout the night.	
"	12/11/17	-	Morning very quiet. Weather excellent with heavy mist. Took over four guns from 62nd Coy, having now 18 guns. Went round	

A7092 Wt. W12839/M1293 750,000. 1/17. D. D & L. Ltd. Forms/C2118/14.

Instructions regarding War Diaries and Intelligence Summaries are contained in F. S. Regs., Part II. and the Staff Manual respectively. Title pages will be prepared in manuscript.

WAR DIARY
or
INTELLIGENCE SUMMARY.
(Erase heading not required.)

(5.)

Army Form C. 2118.

Place	Date	Hour	Summary of Events and Information	Remarks and references to Appendices
In the Line.			the new positions + visited all barrage guns. Arranged [illegible] + laid out amended S.O.S. lines in accordance with D.M.G.O's instructions. Harrassing fire continued. Went round front line guns + found conditions very bad. Rains had made trenches impassable in many places. Situation was quiet. 1 O.R. wounded.	
"	13/11/17	-	Exceptionally quiet morning after gas shell bombardment from 1.15 am. to 1.30 am. Heavy mist. Enemy artillery activity between 9 + 11 am. Issued Op. Orders for relief on 14th inst. Visited NOORDEMDHOEK guns. All work completed. 2/Lt. Edmundson reported for duty from Base. 2nd/Command made necessary administration arrangements with 4th N.Z. M.G. Coy. re relief.	
"	14/11/17	-	Relieving company delayed 3 hrs. but mist heavy so that relief was carried out without incident + completed at 1 p.m. the N.Z. Coy. would not take over belt boxes a special carrying party had to be organised to carry out 200 boxes. Company complete in camp at 4 p.m. except carrying party which did not finish till 7 p.m. Remained in ANZAC CAMP overnight.	
"	15/11/17	-	Pack train to line at 4 am. to bring out belt boxes. Coy. paraded at 8.45 am. + marched via LA CLYTTE to WESTOUTRE. Advance party under Lt. Leslie preceded the Coy. + had hot meal in preparation when Coy.	

A7092 Wt. W128.9/M1293. 750,000. 1/17. D. D & L. Ltd. Forms/C2118/14.

Instructions regarding War Diaries and Intelligence Summaries are contained in F. S. Regs., Part II. and the Staff Manual respectively. Title pages will be prepared in manuscript.

WAR DIARY
or
INTELLIGENCE SUMMARY.

(Erase heading not required.)

Army Form C. 2118.

Place	Date	Hour	Summary of Events and Information	Remarks and references to Appendices
			arrived. This was adopted daily during the march south & answered admirably. Marching was bad chiefly owing to the congested traffic on the roads. Arrived in new camp at 1pm. & found conditions very bad. The ground was a field of mud. & the tents were mostly uninhabitable. Fatigues during afternoon cleaning camp & sandbagging tents. Attended Bg. conference at Bg. Hq. at 3pm. Reorganisation discussed.	
WESTOUTRE	16/11/17	-	Day devoted to cleaning of guns, equipment etc. Bag parade at 3pm. Men in good spirits though conditions were exceedingly bad. Attached infantry returned to units. 4 O.R. proceeded on leave to U.K.	
"	17/11/17	-	Company paraded at 8.30 am. & proceeded by route march to VIEUX BERQUIN area. Roads clear & marching therefore much improved. Transport accompanied the unit. Weather excellent. All halts at 10 mins. to the hour. Marched for five hours & arrived in new billets at 2pm. Excellent accomodation for all ranks. Company quickly settled down.	
VIEUX BERQUIN AREA (WEST)				
"	18/11/17	-	Company moved to BUSNES area. Paraded 9.45 am. Routine of move well carried out, advance party moving off to time under Lt. Stevenson & billeting party under Lt. Colley. Packing of limbers well carried out. Weather conditions excellent & all ranks in splendid spirits. March discipline greatly improved. Arrived in billets at	
BUSNES AREA (EAST)				

A7092 Wt. W12839/M1293 750,000. 1/17. D. D & L. Ltd. Forms/C2118/14.

WAR DIARY
or
INTELLIGENCE SUMMARY.
(Erase heading not required.)

Army Form C. 2118.

Instructions regarding War Diaries and Intelligence Summaries are contained in F. S. Regs., Part II. and the Staff Manual respectively. Title pages will be prepared in manuscript.

Place	Date	Hour	Summary of Events and Information	Remarks and references to Appendices
			9.30pm. Excellent billets. Very few cases of sickness amongst the men.	
BISNES AREA	19/11/17	–	Marched to BARLIN AREA VIA HALLICOURT. Paraded at 8.30 am. Billeting & advance parties as usual. Conditions still good. Arrived BARLIN at 2pm.	
BARLIN.			Foot inspection at 3pm. + limber cleaning at 3.30pm.	
	20/11/17	–	Moved to MONT ST. ELOI. Transport brigaded + moved independently.	
ST. ELOI.			Coy. parade 9.30 am. + arrived ST. ELOI at 1.30pm. Rain threatening.	
MAREUIL.	21/11/17	–	Moved to MAREUIL. Excellent billets for all ranks. After five days marching the men were in excellent spirits + looked very fit.	
"	22/11/17	–	9am. – 9.30am. Physical Training } The remainder of the day was devoted to 9.45am. – 10.15am. Squad Drill } cleaning equipment + to compiling lists of deficiencies for indents. Attended Bde. conference at 3pm. re training for ensuing month.	
"	23/11/17	–	Parades as for 22nd inst. Baths arranged for all ranks. Submitted training programme for next week (see appendix). Made reconnaissance of GAVRELLE SECTOR in accordance with G.O.C.s instructions with a view to action should the enemy retire on the front. Visited Coy. Hq. 92nd M.G.Coy. [illegible] the area. Arranged for guides for Section Officers next day.	APPENDIX "B".

A7092. Wt. W128_9/M1293. 750,000. 1/17. D. D & L. Ltd. Forms/C2118/14.

Instructions regarding War Diaries and Intelligence Summaries are contained in F. S. Regs., Part II. and the Staff Manual respectively. Title pages will be prepared in manuscript.

WAR DIARY
or
INTELLIGENCE SUMMARY.
(Erase heading not required.)

Army Form C. 2118.

(8)

Place	Date	Hour	Summary of Events and Information	Remarks and references to Appendices
MARDEUIL.	24/11/17	-	Cleaning up of stores etc. continued. Section Officers made reconnaissance of GAVRELLE SECTOR. Drafted scheme for action of company in event of enemy retiral.	
"	25/11/17	-	Church parades for all denominations. Sub Section Officers reconnoitred line & made complete personal reconnaissance of GAVRELLE & OPPY sectors during the day. Amended scheme for advance accordingly & submitted same to Bgde. (see Appendix).	APPENDIX "C".
"	26/11/17	-	Inspection of Transport by O.C. Divisional Train. Condition of animals & vehicles reported satisfactory but harness requires work. Parades etc. as per programme. Transport moved to TRAFALGAR CAMP to cover standings during afternoon. Visited Bge. & D.A.D.O.S. re supplies etc.	
"	27/11/17	-	Parades as per programme. Inspected billets & camp area & found everything in excellent order. Visited No. 5 Squadron R.F.C. for instruction in the possibilities of aerial photography as a means of locating M.Gs. Class in Guard Mounting for junior N.C.O.s. under C.S.M.	
"	28/11/17	-	Nos. 1 & 2 Secs. on range testing Guns & practising drill in holding & stoppages. Programme altered in view of probable move to new area. Inspected Nos. 3 & 4 Secs. & Hq. section. Very good parade. Equipment clean but badly fitted. All ranks	

A7092. Wt. W12839/M1293. 750,000. 1/17. D. D & L. Ltd. Forms/C2118/14.

Instructions regarding War Diaries and Intelligence Summaries are contained in F. S. Regs., Part II. and the Staff Manual respectively. Title pages will be prepared in manuscript.

WAR DIARY
or
INTELLIGENCE SUMMARY.
(Erase heading not required.)

Army Form C. 2118.

(9)

Place	Date	Hour	Summary of Events and Information	Remarks and references to Appendices
			looked fit + smart. Inspected Transport personnel at 3pm. Exceptional turn out; men smart + clean, equipment up to date + general appearance excellent.	
MAROEUIL	29/11/17	-	Inspected Nos. 1+2 Sects.: Very satisfactory parade. Nos. III + IV on range. Inspection of box respirators during afternoon by Divisional Gas N.C.O.	
"	30/11/17	-	Parades as per programme together with baths for all ranks. Administrative Instructions for move to new area received + necessary arrangements made. Warned at 3pm. to be ready to move immediately. Issued necessary instructions. Limbers packed etc. Entrained at MAROEUIL STATION at 10pm. Eighty limbers accompanied Coy.; Remainder of Transport following by road left at 7.30pm. for BAPAUME. Detraining station for Coy. TINCOURT.	

Jas. Chalmers Capt.
Cmdg. 62 M.G. Coy

A7092. Wt. W128_g/M1293 750,000. 1/17. D. D & L. Ltd. Forms/C2118/14.

APPENDIX – "A". War Diary

SECRET. Copy No. 11.

53 Machine Gun Company Operation Order No.111.

Maps:-

BELGIUM & FRANCE, SHEET 28.

[illegible].

All Sheets showing POLYGON WOOD.

---

1. 53 M.G.Company will relieve 110 M.G.Company on the morning of the 5/11/17 in the positions at present occupied by that Company N. of POLYGON WOOD, in Left Brigade Sector.

2. No. 1 Section under Lieut. [illegible] will take over four positions in [illegible] Group.
One Sub-Section of No. 2 Section under Lieut. [illegible] will relieve the two front line guns on right battalion front. Remaining Sub-Section will be at [illegible] Line.
No. 3 Section under 2/Lieut. JACK will relieve H.Q. Group.
No. 4 Section under 2/Lieut. GODDARD will relieve Section in JETTY WOOD.
Nos. 3 & 4 Sections will take part in operations on the 6th inst. Details have been issued to Officers concerned.
Transport will remain in its present position in Camp [illegible].30.c.7.9. Sheet 28.

3. COMMUNICATIONS.
For messages between Coy.H.Q. in POLYGON WOOD and Transport lines existing relay posts will be relieved at [illegible] in POLYGON WOOD, Left Brigade H.Q. in HOOGE CRATER, and at School in I.[illegible].c. Sheet 28.

4. S.O.S. Signals will be taken over from relieved Company.

5. One R.A.M.C. Orderly will be at Coy. H.Q., and one with No.1 Section. Positions of First Aid Posts to be taken over from 110 Company.

6. Coy.H.Q. at J.10.b.10.90. Brigade H.Q. in HOOGE CRATER.

7. Completion of relief to be reported to Coy.H.Q. by runner.

(Sd) J Boswell Lieut. & Adjt.,
53rd Machine Gun Company.

DISTRIBUTION.

Copy No.1	..	Bde. Major.
2.	..	D.M.G.O.
3	..	O.C., Coy.
4	..	O.C.No.1 Section.
5	..	" " 2 "
6	..	" " 3 "
7	..	" " 4 "
8	..	Transport Officer.
9	..	110 M.G.Coy.
10	..	File.
11 & 12		War Diary.

Copy No. 8

APPENDICES.

No. 1. One Sub-Section of No. 2, Nos. 1, 3 & 4 Sections, and H.Q. Details will move off from Transport Lines in that order at 4.30 a.m. 5/11/17 - Dress, fighting order with greatcoats - and will travel as far as HELL FIRE CORNER in limbers; thence by Sections at five minutes interval to BUTTE in POLYGON WOOD, where guides will meet relieving Sections at 7 a.m.

No. 2. Everything except guns and spare parts will be taken over from relieved Company. Copies of receipts willbe sent to Coy. H.Q.

No. 3. Sections will take up two days rations and water.

No. 4. Gun teams will consist of one N.C.O. and four men. One Sergeant per Section will go into the line.

No. 5. Sections taking part in operations on the 6th inst. will carry in all material required for barrage purposes.

J Boswell

Lieut. & Adjt.,
62nd Machine Gun Company.

DISTRIBUTION.

Copy No. 1 .. O.C. Coy.
2 .. O.C. No.1 Section.
3 .. " " 2 "
4 .. " " 3 "
5 .. " " 4 "
6 .. Transport Officer.
7 .. File.
8 & 9. War Diary.

APPENDIX "B"

62nd Company – Machine Gun Compy. Training Programme. 26/11/17 – 1/12/17.

Date	9 A.M.	9.15 A.M. – 10 A.M.	10 A.M. – 10.30 A.M.	11 A.M. – 11.30 A.M.	11.30 A.M. – 12 NOON	12 NOON – 12.30 P.M.	12.30 P.M. – 1 P.M.	2.30 P.M. – 4 P.M.	Lectures	Remarks
Monday 26th Novr.	Section Inspections	Squad & Company Drill	Physical Training	Stripping	Mechanism	Stoppages	Elementary Gun Drill	Recreation	–	Special attention will be paid
Tuesday 27th Novr.	Section Inspections	Squad & Company Drill	Physical Training	Stripping	Mechanism	Stoppages	Elementary Gun Drill	Recreation	To N.C.Os at 2.30 pm. by C.O. Subj: Discipline	throughout to:- (1) The training of N.C.Os
Wednesday 28th Novr.	Section Inspections	C.O's Inspection (Of Personnel)	Physical Training	Spare Parts where kept and how fitted	The mechanism of the Belt Filling machine	Prolonged Stoppages and Repairs	Casualty Drill	Recreation	–	(2) The training of new drafts. (3) The training
Thursday 29th Novr.	Section Inspections	Squad & Company Drill	Physical Training	Spare Parts where kept and how fitted	The mechanism of the Belt Filling machine	Prolonged Stoppages and Repairs	Casualty Drill	Gas Appliance Inspection by Div. Gas Off at 2 pm.	–	of every N.C.O. and gun number in the work of the
Friday 30th Novr.	Section Inspections	Squad & Company Drill	Physical Training	Stripping	Mechanism	Stoppages	Advanced Gun Drill	Recreation	–	N.C.O. or number above him.
Saturday 1st Decr.	Section Inspections	C.O's Inspection (Of Gun Equipment)	Physical Training	Stripping	Mechanism	Stoppages	Advanced Gun Drill	Recreation	–	

(Signed) J. Boswell. Lieut & Adjt for O.C.
62nd Machine Gun Coy.

APPENDIX "C"

62 COY. MACHINE GUN CORPS.

Suggested scheme for Tactical use of Machine Guns in connection with 62nd Inf. Bde. Instructions No. 1 dated 23/11/17.

<u>The probable conditions are:-</u>

(a) The enemy will be retiring, and consequently will be fighting a rearguard action.

(b) Opposition will consist of isolated M.Gs., snipers and small infantry detachments. A holding attack may be expected.

(c) Contours are roughly parallel to the line of advance.

(d) In the event of a successful advance, the distance to be carried is a long one.

(e) Infantry battalions are numerically weak.

(f) Artillery support will be relatively small.

Under these conditions, the rôle of the Vickers guns must be defensive. Any targets occurring during the advance can be dealt with by rifle and Lewis gun fire, and by bombing. Should consolidation be necessary on an intermediate line, however, or should the enemy deliver a holding attack, the weakness of our force will become apparent. The Vickers guns will then have to supply a large volume of fire to counterbalance the small number of rifles available, and to supplement the artillery. The defence of the captured area will therefore devolve upon the machine guns. This will result whether the rôle of the Brigade be as laid down in (a) (b) or (c), para 2. of Bde. Instructions No. 1.

Disposition should therefore be made accordingly: I beg to submit the following scheme:-

On the principle that in defence machine guns are best echeloned in depth, I would propose disposing the guns of this Company in three lines as follows:-

<u>1st Line.</u> Three detachments of two guns each. These would advance with the infantry supports. The left detachment would follow the spur through G.13 and 14 central, the centre detachment the spur through G.20 central, and the right detachment the line due East through SQUARE WOOD. Should an intermediate line have to be consolidated, these guns are at any point of the advance in the best positions for their Officers to observe the situation, and to take action on the same lines as are proposed for the defence of the final objective. Should the BLUE LINE be taken, the left detachment would take up position in the vicinity of G.15.a.30.00 with battle lines on a bearing of 132° Mag; the centre detachment would be sited in the vicinity of G.21.b.central with battle line on a bearing of 12° Mag; the right detachment would take up position near G.29.c.10.10, one gun with battle lines along the N.W. edge of CLOSTER WOOD, and the other on a bearing of 16° Mag.

<u>2nd Line.</u> One Section of four guns and a detachment of two guns. The Section of four guns would move along the same route as the

(centre

centre detachment of the 1st Line. Should the advance be held up, it would at once take up a defensive position. Its final position in a successful advance would be in the vicinity of C.20.b.50.30, from which position two guns would engage the sunken road through C.13 central, and two guns the sunken roads from C.13.d.30.00 to C.13.d.40.60. Should a gun of the centre or left front line detachments be put out of action, its place would immediately be taken by a gun from this group. Casualties to personnel would be replaced in the same way. Similarly, a detachment of two guns would advance behind the right forward detachment, forming a defensive point at any time, and ultimately taking up position in the vicinity of C.27.b.30.10, from which position it would engage the group of dugouts around C.28.d.00.60. This detachment would also act as reserve for the right front line guns, as in the previous case.

<u>3rd Line.</u> One Section of four guns would remain in Company reserve, and be utilised as required. Two teams would be kept intact as a mobile reserve, while the other two would be used to replace casualties forward. In the final stage, Company H.Q., together with this reserve would be in the vicinity of C.19.d.05.90.

By such a scheme the work of all guns is co-ordinated. The carrying out of the work would be on the lines indicated in my September - October Report, page 2, para. 2. Ammunition, rations and water supply would be done by the Company, and the administration of the unit would not be complicated as is the case when the Company is broken up. The only real difficulty in the way is the inevitable one of "carriers". Each pair of guns in the first and second lines would require 1 N.C.O. and 5 men as a carrying party. Only with these would sufficient ammunition be taken forward: without this only 75 % of the guns could go into action.

Appended is a map illustrating the above scheme.

[signature] Capt.,
Commanding 32nd Machine Gun Company.

23/11/17.

Instructions regarding War Diaries and Intelligence Summaries are contained in F. S. Regs., Part II. and the Staff Manual respectively. Title pages will be prepared in manuscript.

WAR DIARY
or
INTELLIGENCE SUMMARY.
(Erase heading not required.)

Army Form C. 2118.

Dec 1917 (1.) 62nd Bde. M.G. C. Vol 22

Place	Date	Hour	Summary of Events and Information	Remarks and references to Appendices
PERONNE	1/12/17	-	Detrained at PERONNE at 8am. & marched to CARTIGNY arriving at 11 am. Billetted in huts & cellars. Fighting limbers followed arriving at 2pm. Filled guns & prepared for move at short notice. Remainder of transport moving by road arrived at 7pm. Learned that enemy had attacked south of CAMBRAI; other two Brigades of Division had gone straight into line.	
CARTIGNY	2/12/17	-	Morning devoted to cleaning camp etc. Warned at 1pm to be ready to move during the afternoon. Made preparations accordingly. Move cancelled.	
"	3/12/17	-	Warned to move at 2pm. Made preparations accordingly. Company marched to LONGUEVESNES. Men billetted in huts; officers under canvas. Village full of cavalry. C.O. made reconnaissance of proposed defensive line in conjunction with Battn. C.O.s. Decided action in case of enemy success on either flank.	
LONGUEVESNES	4/12/17	-	C.O. & Section Officers made detailed reconnaissance of defensive position. Gun positions decided & allocation of sections made. Scheme explained at officers' conference. Company devoted day to gun cleaning & fixing new camp. Men very comfortable but transport out	

(A7092). Wt. W12839/M1293. 750,000. 1/17. D. D. & L. Ltd. Forms/C.2118/14.

Instructions regarding War Diaries and Intelligence Summaries are contained in F. S. Regs., Part II. and the Staff Manual respectively. Title pages will be prepared in manuscript.

WAR DIARY
or
INTELLIGENCE SUMMARY.
(Erase heading not required.)

Army Form C. 2118.

(8)

Place	Date	Hour	Summary of Events and Information	Remarks and references to Appendices
			in the open + facilities poor. Weather extremely cold. Warned to be ready to move at 15 min. notice between the hours of 6am. + 8am. daily. Issued orders for 6am. parade accordingly.	
LONGUEVESNES	5/12/17	-	"Stand To" at 6am. All ranks on parade in fighting order. Guns kept ready for action. P.T., Coy. Drill, + general training carried out during the day. Sub Section Officers made reconnaissance of defensive line.	
"	6/12/17	-	"Stand To" 6am. P.T. Coy. Drill + Training during the morning. Afternoon devoted to recreation. Weather conditions excellent but animals suffering from exposure.	
	7/12/17	-	Parades as on 6th inst. C.O. made reconnaissance of front system of Left Bge. area with view to relief of 64th Coy. in that area. Got dispositions from O.C. 64th Coy. + went round line. Conditions very quiet NO MAN'S LAND being apparently very wide at this point. Wiring + digging the only activities in the line. Excellent country for M.Gs.	

(A7092). Wt. W12839/M1293. 750,000. 1/17. D.D. & L., Ltd. Forms/C.2118/14.

Instructions regarding War Diaries and Intelligence Summaries are contained in F. S. Regs., Part II. and the Staff Manual respectively. Title pages will be prepared in manuscript.

WAR DIARY
or
INTELLIGENCE SUMMARY.
(Erase heading not required.)

(3)

Army Form C. 2118.

Place	Date	Hour	Summary of Events and Information	Remarks and references to Appendices
LONGUEVESNES	8/12/17	-	Coy. at training as on previous days. C.O. reported to D.M.G.O. at Divisional Hq. + received instructions with reference to reliefs. Thaw succeeded the frost making camp conditions very bad. One section attached to 64th Coy in the line for duty.	
"	9/12/17	-	Coy. at training as above. 2nd/command + O.C. Transport went to HEAUDECOURT to arrange taking over of accommodation from 64th Coy. Relief orders received from D.M.G.O. Arranged details with O.C. 64th Coy.	
In the Line.	10/12/17	-	Relieved 64th M.G. Coy. in Left Sector of Divisional Area. Coy. paraded at 10.45 a.m. + arrived advanced Hq. at 12.15 p.m. Guides waiting to take teams in. Relief complete by 3 p.m. without incident. All guns of the Coy. in the line together with 4 guns of 64th Coy. left under my command making 20 guns in all. Conditions very quiet. Guns scattered, no definite scheme having yet been decided. Went round guns of attached section + made arrangements for progress of work. Rear Hq. at HEAUDECOURT: animals now under cover.	
"	11/12/17	.	Misty day making movement over the open simpler. Succeeded	

(A7092). Wt. W12839/M1293 750,000. 1/17. D. D. & L., Ltd. Forms/C.2118/14

Instructions regarding War Diaries and Intelligence Summaries are contained in F. S. Regs., Part II. and the Staff Manual respectively. Title pages will be prepared in manuscript.

WAR DIARY
or
INTELLIGENCE SUMMARY.

(Erase heading not required.)

Army Form C. 2118.

(4)

Place	Date	Hour	Summary of Events and Information	Remarks and references to Appendices
			in getting round all guns. Organised work. Checked S.O.S. lines.	
In the line.	12/12/17	-	Round line with D.M.G.O. Various changes in gun positions decided on. Infantry now digging a fixed line for defence ~~[illegible]~~ same thereby making situation clear for M.G. defence. Arranged for necessary changes in guns. Reported to O.C. Battns.	
"	13/12/17	-	Visited all guns with Section Officers. Arranged for R.E. assistance in putting in shelters in saps behind positions. Decided on necessary alterations in emplacements & improvements to existing accommodation. Officers conference at Coy. Hq. Situation dealt with & aeroplane photos issued with orders for use in barrage fire. Work progressed. No interference from the enemy, everything being abnormally quiet.	
"	14/12/17	-	Round line with G.O.C. Bde., Battn. Commanders & D.M.G.O. Further changes in positions decided on. In consequence the work to be undertaken has been doubled. Issued orders to meet the position & organised labour as far as possible.	

(A7092). Wt. W12839/M1293 75,000. 1/17. D. D. & L., Ltd. Forms/C.2118/14.

Instructions regarding War Diaries and Intelligence Summaries are contained in F. S. Regs., Part II. and the Staff Manual respectively. Title pages will be prepared in manuscript.

WAR DIARY
or
INTELLIGENCE SUMMARY.
(Erase heading not required.)

(5)

Army Form C. 2118.

Place	Date	Hour	Summary of Events and Information	Remarks and references to Appendices
			Opportune arrival of draft of 170 O.R. helped considerably. Increased trench strength by every available man. Hand labour by carrying in water & rations by pack animal up to gun positions. Organised day work as far as possible but had to stop owing to visibility at some positions & resort to night work.	
In the field.	15/12/17	-	Visited all guns & settled details of new position with section officers. Relieved officers by sub-section officers during afternoon. Work progressed. Carried out harassing fire from three guns. Engaged enemy aeroplane at 10 a.m. Position quiet & line apparently being consolidated by both parties.	
"	16/12/17	-	Rearranged teams to get sections under their own officers & regrouped so as to get two sections in front line & two in reserve for purposes of relief. Received instructions re new S.O.S. line from D.M.G.O. Made necessary calculations putting ~~eight~~ ten guns on S.O.S. line. Order boards & number boards to hand from pioneers. Issued	

(A7092). Wt. W12839/M1293. 750,000. 1/17. D. D. & L., Ltd. Forms/C.2118/14.

Instructions regarding War Diaries and Intelligence Summaries are contained in F. S. Regs., Part II. and the Staff Manual respectively. Title pages will be prepared in manuscript.

WAR DIARY
or
INTELLIGENCE SUMMARY.
(Erase heading not required.)

(6)

Army Form C. 2118.

Place	Date	Hour	Summary of Events and Information	Remarks and references to Appendices
			these & all guns. Rangecards made for all positions. Work continued on shelters & on saps in conjunction with R.Es. Harrassing fire carried out during the night. Carried out a shoot from 7.30pm. to 7.47pm. in co-operation with artillery on suspected enemy relief. 30,000 rds. fired by eight guns. Enemy retaliation very slight.	
In the field.	17/12/17	.	Work continued on all emplacements & shelters. Duckboards sent up & laid at each position. Went round all sections & checked battery & S.O.S. lines. Arranged relief for 18th inst. with O.C. 64th Coy. in accordance with instructions from D.M.G.O. Harrassing fire carried out throughout the night. 2nd/command made reconnaissance in accordance with Defence Scheme issued by D.M.G.O. in view of possible enemy attack.	
"	18/12/17	.	Spent day in office work. Sector now thoroughly organised & in working order. A few days work will complete arrangements. Issued Operation Order for relief. One section remaining attached to 64th Coy. on S.O.S. guns. Company to HEAUDECOURT.	

(A7092). Wt. W12839/M1293 750,000. 1/17. D. D. & L., Ltd. Forms/C.2118/14.

Instructions regarding War Diaries and Intelligence Summaries are contained in F. S. Regs., Part II. and the Staff Manual respectively. Title pages will be prepared in manuscript.

WAR DIARY
or
INTELLIGENCE SUMMARY.
(Erase heading not required.)

Army Form C. 2118.

(7)

Place	Date	Hour	Summary of Events and Information	Remarks and references to Appendices
HEUDECOURT	19/12/17		CAPT J. CHALMERS proceeded on 30 days leave to ENGLAND. LIEUT T. BUSWELL took command. Company carried on with general cleaning, lists of deficiencies in all equipment being taken	
"	20/12/17		General training. Outdoor training interfered with by heavy frost & snow. Lectures by section officers was the chief parade.	
"	21/12/17		General training. Section officers reconnoitred ground in rear of Division trench system for defence in case of enemy break through. Two officers went for 1 day's leave to AMIENS	
"	22/12/17		General training. NO 1 Section prepared to go in the line to relieve NO 3 Section in reserve positions. CO inspected transport.	
	23/12/17		Training as usual. NO 1 Section relieved NO 3 Section & came under the command of OC 64 Company. LIEUT G LESLIE & 2 OR's went on leave to U.K.	
	24/12/17		Training. CO & sub-section officers reconnoitred ground mentioned on 21/12/17. CO visited OC 64 Company in the line & made arrangements for relief on 26/12/17. ~~Comp~~	
	25/12/17		Christmas Day. No parades. D M G O visited Company. Company had special dinner. CO visited NO 1 Section in the line.	

(A7092). Wt. W12839/M1293 75,000. 1/17. D. D. & L., Ltd. Forms/C.2118/14.

Army Form C. 2118.

Instructions regarding War Diaries and Intelligence Summaries are contained in F. S. Regs., Part II. and the Staff Manual respectively. Title pages will be prepared in manuscript.

WAR DIARY
or
INTELLIGENCE SUMMARY.

(Erase heading not required.)

(8)

Place	Date	Hour	Summary of Events and Information	Remarks and references to Appendices
In the line	26/12/17		Company relieved 64th Company (less one section attached to this company) in the line, Company H.Q. on Railway between HEUDECOURT & PEIZIERES. Relief uneventful & completed by 4.15 pm. 2000 rounds fired on enemy communications in VILLERS-GUISLAIN.	
"	27/12/17		D.M.G.O. visited Company HQ. Programme of work settled. CO went round line. Section officers received programme of work. All work hindered greatly by snow & frost. Difficulty with guns because of frost although all kept in working order. 7000 rounds fired against enemy working parties. Very slight enemy activity.	
"	28/12/17		Heavy blizzard. Snowdrifts filled in all emplacements & rendered firing difficult. Work interfered with. CO went round all guns. Positions of guns accurately determined. Fired 5000 rounds at enemy communications. Enemy activity slight.	
"	29/12/17		Slight thaw enabled work to be carried on more rapidly. No difficulty with guns. 12000 rounds fired at enemy communications. Little hostile activity.	
	30/12/17		CO went round line with Brigadier & D.M.G.O. New gun positions sited. Enemy shelling much above normal between 6 am & 7 am. 7000 rounds fired.	

Instructions regarding War Diaries and Intelligence Summaries are contained in F. S. Regs., Part II. and the Staff Manual respectively. Title pages will be prepared in manuscript.

WAR DIARY
or
INTELLIGENCE SUMMARY.
(Erase heading not required.)

(9)

Army Form C. 2118.

Place	Date	Hour	Summary of Events and Information	Remarks and references to Appendices
In the line	31/12/17		Four guns taken out of the line from various places. Section of 64' Company relieved & joined remainder of 64 Company at HEUDECOURT. There are ~~see~~ now 15 guns actually in the line for defence of the line with a sixteenth doing Anti Aircraft work at Coy H.Q instead of 20. New S.O.S lines put on all guns doing S.O.S work. Work on new positions started. At 12 midnight 31/12/17–1/1/18 9 guns opened fire, firing one belt each, at points behind enemy line.	

W H Stephenson Lt & A/Capt
62 Machine Gun Coy

(A7092). Wt. W12839/M1293 750,000 1/17. D. D. & L., Ltd. Forms/C.2118/14.

War Diary

62nd Machine Gun Company.

Monthly Report for month ending 30/11/17.

The feature of the month has been the movement of the Company from YPRES to PERONNE. Other than this, routine has been normal and has not offered opportunity for fresh tactical or technical lessons. The experiences of the month simply accentuate points which have already been repeatedly brought to notice.

1. During the five days march from YPRES to MAROEUIL, the need of a G.S.Wagon other than that attached to A.S.C. was apparent. With it an M.G.Company would be altogether independent of that most unreliable branch of the Service – the Motor Transport.

2. The real need for a field kitchen was again impressed on all officers. The adequate preparation of the men's food is the great difficulty of an M.G.Companyon the march.

3. Since coming into the line at PEIZIERE, M.G.Officers have again been impressed by the fact that a "garrison" front is the best training ground for Machine Gunners. No range behind the lines can give the facilities enjoyed in such a place as this. Action in the open, harassing fire, battery shoots, practise stoppages: indeed everything that is most needed in a Gunner's training can be got here. Not, however, until the M.G.Officer has as free a hand as the Artillery Officer in arranging his shoots can the full advantage be taken of these opportunities of training all gun numbers, and of making spare numbers quite capable of replacing the more experienced Gunners in the event of casualties.

(Sd.) J. Chalmers Capt.
Comdg. 62 Machine Gun Coy

62nd Coy. M. G. Corps		Secret

Operation Order No. 122		Copy No.

1. The Company will be relieved by 64 Coy. M.G.C. on the 18th inst.

2. (a) One guide per team from Nos. 1 and 4 Sections will be at Company Headquarters at 2.30 p.m.

(b) One guide per team from No. 2 Section will be at section headquarters in Sunken Road at W.18 d. 20.30 at 2.30 p.m.

(c) No. 3 Section will be relieved under orders issued separately and will on relief, become the section in reserve attached to 64 Coy. This section will come under orders of O.C. 64 Coy. on completion of company relief.

(d) Guides must know the numbers of the positions from which they come.

3. The following will be handed over to incoming unit:-
(a) Tripods, (b) Belt Boxes, (c) Sentry's Orders and range cards, (d) Trench stores.

"List of Trench Stores" duly countersigned will be rendered to Orderly Room.

4. Section Officers will delay the relief of exposed guns till dusk.

5. Limbers will report as follows:-
(a) One limber to No. 1 Section H.Q. at 2.45 p.m.
(b) One limber to No. 4 Section ration dump at 3 p.m.
(c) One limber to No. 2 Section H.Q. at dusk.
(d) One limber to Coy. H.Q. at 2 p.m.

6. On relief, sections will return to Heudicourt. The Adjutant will arrange for sections to be met and guided to their respective billets.

7. "Relief complete" will be reported to Coy. H.Q. by section Officers.

8. Attention is drawn to 'Trench Standing Orders' re "Reliefs".

17.12.17

(Signed) J. Chalmers, Capt.
Comdg. 62nd M. G. Coy.

APPENDIX to Provisional Machine Gun Scheme submitted 3-12-17.

The detailed reconnaissance carried out today supported the Scheme already suggested. The crests of all spurs have been left to the Lewis Guns as in all cases they offer a restricted field of fire. Forward guns have been so disposed that so long as the infantry line is maintained, fire is either direct enfilade from a flank, or overhead fire from the shoulders of the spurs. Lines of fire have been crossed as far as possible, and provision has been made for the forward slopes of the spurs, which are dead ground to the Lewis guns, being commanded by machine gun fire. All guns from which the initial fire is overhead have been given alternative positions in the valleys to which they will move in the event of the infantry withdrawing. From these alternative positions grazing fire can be maintained along the low ground, and the slopes of the spurs swept.

The siting of flank guns has been given special attention, and in each case the reserve guns have been advanced slightly to positions from which observation of the ground in front of the infantry line can be more easily obtained.

With reference to para (A), the forward guns are sited approximately at the following map references:-

W. 22. c. 20.70
W. 22. c. 90.30
W. 28. b. 80.80
W. 23. c. 30.50
W. 23. c. 80.00
W. 29. b. 30.60
W. 30. a. 15.20
W. 30. a. 95.50

The detachment on the left flank has been advanced to W 21. d. 00. 25 approximately, but retains its original position as an alternative. The reserve guns have been moved forward to

W. 27. d. 3 0   W. 28. b. 3 1.
W. 28. a. 1 1.   W. 28. d. 9 9.

With reference to para (B), the map references of the detachments on the flanks of the Northumberland Fusiliers are:-

One detachment .. F 7. a. 7 7.
One detachment .. F 7. c. 35. 20.

The battery in E. 11. and the detachments in E. 5. and 23 remain as stated. The guns in reserve will be in two detachments at the following references:- E. 5. a. 4 5   E. 4. d. 9 2.
E. 5. c. 7 9   E. 10. b. 3. 8.

Should the situation necessitate rapid movement, arrangements have been made for guns, ammunition and personnel for all forward positions to be sent forward in limbers. It is estimated that these guns can be in action within one hour after leaving camp. The guns will be in position a considerable time before the infantry has arrived, and can be in action if necessary while the infantry is forming. Should it be necessary to withdraw the infantry at a later stage, the guns would remain. All ammunition will be taken up either with the fighting limbers or by pack animal. The need for carrying parties is thereby eliminated. The success of the movement by daylight will depend on the guns getting forward before the enemy is commanding the REVELON RIDGE. Digging in is not essential in any position, ground cover having been chosen. Gun slits however, would immediately be prepared if conditions allowed.

On approval of the above being notified, dispositions of guns will be forwarded to the Battalion Commanders concerned for their information and action with reference to the co-operation with Lewis guns.

J. C. Chalmers Capt.
Comdg. 62nd Machine Gun Coy

4/12/17.

War Diary

Provisional Scheme of M. G. defence in the event of an enemy break through on either flank of the present Divisional Frontage.

Ref. Map Sheets.
57c. S.E. & 62c. N.E.

(A) The Left Flank.

The Company will approach the defensive line allotted by the route through Saulcourt and the road running through E.4 a. & c.

One section of four guns will be located in W.22. c. & d.
One section of four guns will be located in W.23. c. & d. or
W.29 a & b. A detachment of two guns will be disposed in
W.27 a and will be responsible for the left flank of
the line. A detachment of two guns will be disposed in
X 25 a and will be responsible for the right flank.
One section of four guns will engage special targets,
i.e. lines of approach, likely cover etc by overhead
indirect fire from the high ground in W.27. d. and W.28. d.
These guns will also be available for movement to
any necessary point, being directly under the control
of the Company Commander, whose Headquarters will
be in the vicinity of the road junction at W.28. c. 7. 4.

(B) The Right Flank.

The Company will use the approach through Villers and thence to E.12 central.

A detachment of two guns will be disposed in the vicinity of F.1. c 50.00, and will cover the left of the Northumberland Fusiliers. A detachment of two guns will be disposed in the vicinity of F. 7. c. 50.00. from which all approaches to the position occupied by the Northumberland Fusiliers will be commanded.

One section of four guns will be disposed in the vicinity of the Grid line from E 11 central South to E. 11. d. 00. 00, from which position the valleys leading to Epehy and Ste. Emilie are commanded, and a possible withdrawal of the Northumberland Fusiliers could be covered. A detachment of two guns will be disposed near E. 5. d. 00. 50, and will be responsible (for

for the left flank of the Lincoln Regt. situated in E.11.a. A detachment of two guns will be placed in E.23.b. and will be responsible for the right flank of the Queens situated in E 17 a & c.

One section of four guns will be disposed in the high ground in E.10.a. and E.4.d., from which position the exits from Epehy are commanded, and overhead fire can be brought to bear wherever required on the battalion frontages. These guns will also be under the direct control of the Company Commander whose Headquarters will be in the vicinity of E.10c. 60.00. and will therefore be available for movement to any required point.

Reconnaissance

A full reconnaissance of these positions will be made by all Officers concerned on the 4th inst.

O. i/c Transport will reconnoitre the approaches stated, and also alternative routes. He will locate Company Headquarters in each case, and make his own arrangements for delivering ammunition etc: at these points.

3/12/17.

J. Chalmers Capt.
Comdg. 62nd Machine Gun Company.

Secret

Copy No

62nd M. G. Coy.

Operation Order No 90.

1. 62nd M. G. Coy. will relieve 64th M. G. Coy in the line on the 10th inst.

2. No. 2 Section, at present attached 64 Coy. will relieve No. 1 Section of that Coy. in the forward area under arrangements to be made by O.C. 64 Coy. the latter section remaining attached to 62 Coy.

3. Nos. 1, 3 + 4 Sections will parade in that order at five minutes interval, commencing at 10.45 A.M. Headquarters personnel going into the line will move with No. 4 Section.
Dress - fighting order. Orders as to overcoats and jerkins will be issued later.

4. Tripods and belt boxes will be taken over from 64 Coy at the positions. All other gun equipment will be taken in by the Sections.

5. Water. Petrol tins will be taken over as trench stores. In addition 2 filled petrol tins per team will be taken in.

6. Trench Strength. Teams will be one gun commander and four O.R. strong.

7. Guides. One guide per team will meet Sections at the Railway Crossing at W.23 b.10.10. at 12 noon. In all cases, limbers can proceed a considerable distance beyond this point.

8. Allocation. Sections are allocated as follows:-
3 Guns of No. 1 Section under Lieut. Stephenson will relieve 3 guns of No 4 Section 64 Coy. on the right.
4 Guns of No. 4 Section under 2/Lt. Rudkin will relieve 4 guns of No. 2 Section 64 Coy. in the centre.
4 Guns of No. 3 Section and 1 gun of No. 1 Section under 2/Lt. Jacks will relieve No 3 Section 64 Coy. in support.

9. Ammunition. The following minimum will be maintained:-
Belt boxes, filled, ... 14
S.A.A. .... 4000 rounds.

10. S.O.S. The S.O.S. is a rifle grenade bursting into two green and 2 white lights.

11. Rations. The unconsumed portion of the day's rations and rations for the 11th inst. will be carried in. Subsequent arrangements for delivery of rations will be notified to Section Officers.

12. The remainder of the Company will move to Heudicourt at 12 noon under arrangements to be made by the 2nd in Command. Lieut. Leslie will take over 64 Coy's Camp at Heudicourt at 12 noon.

13. Coy. Trench Standing Orders. Pro formas for gun orders, and for daily reports and trench store tables will be issued in due course. Pending this issue, Section Officers will render their daily report to Coy. H.Q. by 8.45 A.M.

14. Transport. Officer i/c Transport will make the necessary arrangements for transport.

15. Completion of relief will be reported to Coy. H.Q. as soon as possible.

9/12/17.

(Signed) [illegible] Boswell [illegible]
62nd Machine Gun Coy.

(P.T.O)

SECRET.

Copy No. 5

62 Machine Gun Coy.
Operation Order No. 221.

1. No. 1 Section will relieve No. 3 Section in the line tomorrow 23rd inst. taking over the same positions.

2. No. 1 Section will parade ready to move off at 9 a.m., and will take in guns, spare parts etc.

3. Tripods, belt boxes, S.A.A. etc. will be taken over from No. 3 Section.

4. All S.O.S. and battle lines will be taken over, and carefully checked.

5. On completion of relief, No. 3 Section will join the Company at HEUDICOURT and take over the billets vacated by No. 1 Section.

6. Relief complete will be reported to Company Orderly Room.

7. The necessary transport for No. 1 Section to be outside the Company Stores by 8.30 a.m. This transport will bring back the guns etc. of No. 3 Section.

W L Stephenson Lt & A/Adjt
62 Machine Gun Coy

APPENDIX.
All precautions will be taken to prevent frostbite and trench feet in the line. O.C. No. 1 Section will ensure that each man takes into the line 3 pairs of socks, and will take with him a supply of whale oil.

[illegible] M.G. Coy. Secret

Operation Order No 251. Copy No.

1. [illegible] will relieve 64 Coy. in the line during the afternoon of 26.12.17.

2. The Coy. rear H.Q. and Transport lines will remain in their present position at HEUDECOURT.

3. Coy. Advanced H.Q. will open at 2 p.m. in the railway cutting at approximately W.2.a.8.1. map sheet 57c. S.E.

4. The Coy. will parade at 1 p.m. and will move off by sections at 1.30 p.m. with five minutes interval between sections. Necessary transport will be at Coy. Stores at 12.45 p.m. Teams will consist of at least 1 N.C.O. and four men.

5. The guns will be divided into four groups viz:–
   (a) Right forward
   (b) Right rear
   (c) Left forward
   (d) Left rear.

6. (a) No. 1 Section under 2/Lt. Shepherd will relieve the positions of the right forward group under orders to be issued by O.C. 64 Coy.
(b) No. 2 Section under 2/Lt. Edmundson will relieve the right rear group.
(c) No. 3 Section under 2/Lt. Jack will relieve the left forward group.
(d) No. 4 Section under 2/Lt. Rudkin will relieve the left rear group.

7. All guns will be relieved by day except No. 1. in the right forward group, and Nos. 4. 5. & 6. in the left forward group. These guns will be relieved according to orders issued to the guides by O.C. 64 Coy.

8. One guide per team for Nos. 3 & 4 Sections will be at the Hq. [illegible] in the sunken road at approximately W.1.B.c.0.2., map sheet 57c S.E., at 2.30 p.m. One guide per team for No. 2 Section will be at Coy. Advanced H.Q. at 2.30 p.m.

9. One team of No. 2 Section will remain at Coy. Advanced H.Q. in reserve.

10. All S.O.S. and [illegible] lines will be taken over and carefully checked.

11. Tripods, belt boxes, S.A.A. etc. will be taken over from 64 Coy.

All trench stores will be taken over and copies of receipts given will be sent to Coy. Advanced H.Q.

"Relief complete" will be reported by runner to Coy. Advanced H.Q.

12. The unexpired portion of rations for 26th will be carried on the man, and the whole of the rations for the 27th if they arrive in time will be taken into the line. If the latter rations do not arrive in time they will be sent up to Coy Advanced H.Q. on mules, and will be met there by guides from each section. The guides will show the transport drivers a what point the rations for subsequent days will be brought.

13 The rations will leave Coy. Stores at 3.00 p.m. each day.

14 Each section will take up six petrol tins of water and on subsequent days 4 tins of water will only be given on receiving a corresponding number of empty ones.

15 Section Officers will take a supply of glycerine into the line.

16 The attention of Section Officers is called to para 6 of to-nights Coy. Orders re posting of sentries.

17 Acknowledge.

W H Stephenson
Lieut. & A/Adjt.
62nd Machine Gun Coy.

Distribution

Copy No 1 ... D.M.G.O.
" " 2 .. 62nd Inf. Bde.
" " 3,4,5,6 - Section Officers.
" " 7 .. O.C. 64 Coy.
" " 8 .. Transport Officer
" " 9 .. C.O.
" " 10 .. File
" " 11 .. War Diary.

Appendix 2

DISPOSITIONS OF OXEN 26/12/17 – 31/12/17.

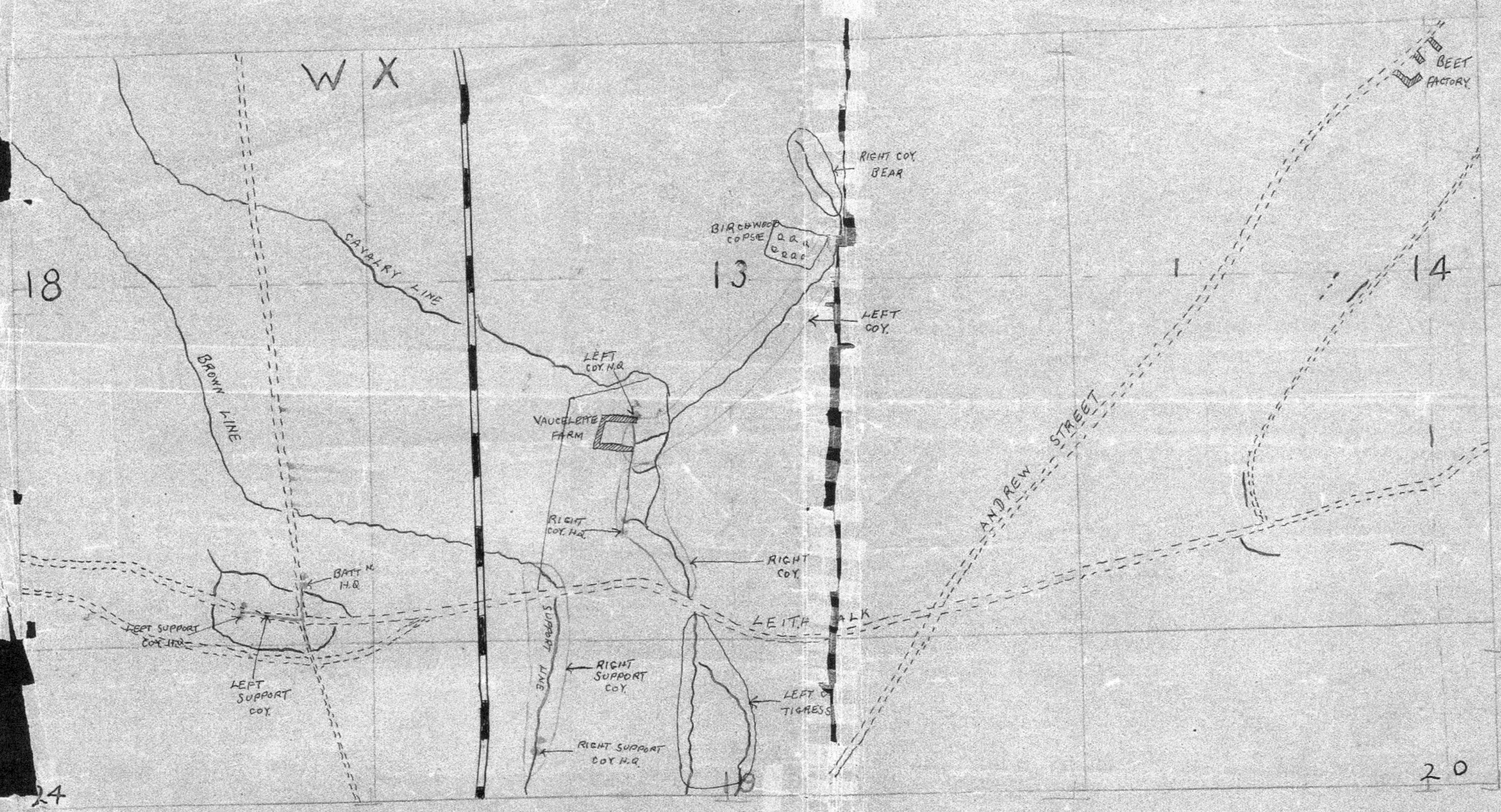

W X

18

13

14

BEET FACTORY

RIGHT COY. BEAR

BIRCHWOOD COPSE

LEFT COY.

LEFT COY. H.Q.

VAUCELETTE FARM

CAVALRY LINE

BROWN LINE

RIGHT COY. H.Q.

RIGHT COY.

ANDREW STREET

LEITH WALK

BATT N. H.Q.

LEFT SUPPORT COY. H.Q.

LEFT SUPPORT COY.

SUPPORT LINE

RIGHT SUPPORT COY.

RIGHT SUPPORT COY. H.Q.

LEFT C[illegible] TIGRESS

24

19

20

SCALE:– 1/5,000

Instructions regarding War Diaries and Intelligence Summaries are contained in F. S. Regs., Part II. and the Staff Manual respectively. Title pages will be prepared in manuscript.

WAR DIARY
or
INTELLIGENCE SUMMARY.
(Erase heading not required.)

Army Form C. 2118.

January 1918 — 62nd Coy M G C — Vol 23

Place	Date	Hour	Summary of Events and Information	Remarks and references to Appendices
[illegible] Field	1/1/18		No unusual activity to mark the New Year. Everything quiet. 5000 rounds fired at enemy communications. O.C. 64 M.G. Company came to advanced Company H.Q. to arrange for relief. Operation orders for relief by 64 Company issued. Issued orders for making & improvement of isolated M.G. positions.	
"	2/1/18		Everything very quiet. 7000 rounds fired at enemy communications near VILLERS GUISLAIN. New positions chosen for two guns.	
"	3/1/18		Everything very quiet. 5000 rounds fired at VILLERS GUISLAIN. Company relieved by 64 M.G. Company & proceeded to HEUDECOURT. Relief completed by 4.30 pm. D.M.G.O. visited Company H.Q. in the morning.	
HEUDECOURT	4/1/18		General cleaning & overhauling of guns & equipment. Programme of work sent to D.M.G.O.	
"	5/1/18		General training. Working party of 1 section sent to help 64 Company. Company stood to at 6 am in accordance with Divisional orders.	
"	6/1/18		General training. CO inspected company & transport. Usual party sent to 64 M.G. Company. Stand to at 6 am.	
"	7/1/18		[illegible] operations orders for company action when in reserve in case of enemy attack issued. Visit by D.M.G.O. company [illegible] with general training. Owing to the ~~[illegible]~~ the [illegible] somewhat of the line the ground has	

(A7092) Wt W12839/M1293 75,000 1/17. D. D. & L., Ltd. Forms/C.2118/14.

93

(2)

WAR DIARY
or
INTELLIGENCE SUMMARY.
(Erase heading not required.)

Army Form C. 2118.

Instructions regarding War Diaries and Intelligence Summaries are contained in F. S. Regs., Part II. and the Staff Manual respectively. Title pages will be prepared in manuscript.

Place	Date	Hour	Summary of Events and Information	Remarks and references to Appendices
			been snow & frost bound, consequently shovelling & carrying which has had to consist chiefly of [illegible]. Work has been done to improve horse lines & render them splinter proof in case of enemy aircraft.	
HEUDECOURT	8/1/18		Stand to at 6 a.m. Party to 64 Company. General training. One section out on tactical scheme – practice of scheme to be put in operation in case of enemy attack. Heavy snow storm interfered with scheme.	
"	9/1/18		O.C. saw O.C. 64 Company re relief on 11/1/18. Company sent to [illegible] section with 64 Company. Lieut WATSON joined up from BASE.	
"	10/1/18		Two sections on tactical scheme – practice of scheme to be put in action in case of enemy attack. Usual working party to the line. O.C. reconnoitred Corps line of defence & issued preliminary O.O. in case of occupation of same being necessary. O.O. for relief issued.	
	11/1/18		In the morning Company prepared for the line. In the afternoon Company relieved 64 Company in the line. Relief complete 4.30 p.m. Company advanced H.Q. again in Railway ~~[illegible]~~ cutting near RAILTON STATION between HEUDECOURT & EPEHY-PEIZIERES	

(A7092) Wt W12839/M1293 75,000. 1/17. D. D. & L., Ltd. Forms/C.2118/14.

Instructions regarding War Diaries and Intelligence Summaries are contained in F. S. Regs., Part II. and the Staff Manual respectively. Title pages will be prepared in manuscript.

WAR DIARY
or
INTELLIGENCE SUMMARY.
(Erase heading not required.)

(3)

Army Form C. 2118.

Place	Date	Hour	Summary of Events and Information	Remarks and references to Appendices
In the line	12/1/18		Day very quiet. Owing to thaw all positions are getting in a very bad state & are falling in notwithstanding all efforts to revet.	
"	13/1/18		Thaw still continuing. All trenches & positions getting worse owing to heavy rain. Fired 2000 rounds at enemy communications. Greater enemy activity both in the air & with artillery.	
"	14/1/18		Much activity of enemy in the air. Fired 1000 rounds at hostile aeroplanes & 4000 rounds at ground targets.	
	15/1/18		Advanced Coy HQ visited by DMGO. Inspected new gun positions. Gale blowing during the day accompanied by heavy showers. Front line trench practically impassable owing to falling in of trench. Fired 8000 rounds at enemy communications & tracks. 2/Lt Jack proceeded on leave to U.K.	
"	16/1/18		Very little hostile activity. Gale continued until evening. Fired 6000 rounds at enemy communications. Did much work on repairing trenches & emplacements.	

(A7092). Wt W12839/M1293. 75,000. 1/17. D. D. & L., Ltd. Forms/C.2118/14.

Instructions regarding War Diaries and Intelligence Summaries are contained in F. S. Regs., Part II. and the Staff Manual respectively. Title pages will be prepared in manuscript.

WAR DIARY
or
INTELLIGENCE SUMMARY.
(Erase heading not required.)

Army Form C. 2118.

(8)

Place	Date	Hour	Summary of Events and Information	Remarks and references to Appendices
L helene	17/1/18		Very little enemy activity probably owing to bad visibility. Fired 5000 rounds at enemy communications. Lad work on [illegible] & emplacements [illegible] a little better. Alternative emplacements for some guns chosen.	
"	18/1/18		Officers of 28 M.G. Company made a reconnaissance of Company sector. Fired 2000 rounds at enemy communications.	
"	19/1/18		Company relieved by 64 M.G. Company & returned to billets in HEUDECOURT.	
"	20/1/18		Baths for company. Day spent in general cleaning. Capt CHALMERS rejoined from leave & took over command of the Company.	

(A7092). Wt W12839/M1293 75,0.0. 1/17. D. D. & L., Ltd. Forms/C.2118/14.

(5)

Army Form C. 2118.

Instructions regarding War Diaries and Intelligence Summaries are contained in F. S. Regs., Part II. and the Staff Manual respectively. Title pages will be prepared in manuscript.

WAR DIARY
or
INTELLIGENCE SUMMARY.
(Erase heading not required.)

Place	Date	Hour	Summary of Events and Information	Remarks and references to Appendices
HEAUDECOURT	20/1/18	–	Day devoted to general cleaning up after coming out of the line. Clothes & equipment in bad condition owing to recent weather & consequent state of trenches but all ranks in good spirits. Comfortable quarters in village & good supplies. C.O. returned from leave.	
"	21/1/18	–	Cleaning continued. Inspections by section officers of all stores etc. & rendering of deficiencies: there was not much to be made up the coy. being well up to date with everything. Fatigues during afternoon putting limb[er] shelter round transport lines. Weather wet & camp very muddy. Fatigue party sent to line for work on new emplacements. Worked on Defence Schemes & issued Operation Order attached.	APPENDIX
"	22/1/18	–	Parades as per programme attached. Formed classes for men according to their state of proficiency. Posted reinforcements to sections; the company now at full strength. Difficulty in revolver supply has occurred as all reinforcements arrive with rifles. Inspected camps & all billets & arranged fatigues to carry out necessary improvements during the afternoon. Inspected transport: animals looking well	APPENDIX

(A7092). Wt. W12839/M1293 75,000. 1/17. D. D. & L., Ltd. Forms/C.2118/14.

Instructions regarding War Diaries and Intelligence Summaries are contained in F. S. Regs., Part II. and the Staff Manual respectively. Title pages will be prepared in manuscript.

WAR DIARY
or
INTELLIGENCE SUMMARY.
(Erase heading not required.)

(6)

Army Form C. 2118.

Place	Date	Hour	Summary of Events and Information	Remarks and references to Appendices
			and apparently now quite recovered from work at YPRES. Horses in good condition & personnel satisfactory. Section officers made reconnaissance in connection with operation order issued yesterday. Rain during evening.	
HEAUDECOURT	23/1/18	-	Great improvement in camp since yesterday. Parades carried out as per programme. Inspected HQ. & No. IV Sections & found a very satisfactory parade; men looked fit & equipment was up to date. Visited gun positions of Defence Scheme "A" with O.C. No. III Section. Fatigues to line & Town Major daily during rest. Camp fatigues during afternoon; cleaning ammn., filling belts, digging bomb protection to huts etc. Paid out the company at 5 p.m.	
"	24/1/18	-	Inspected No. I Section & found excellent turn out. Visited No. I Section positions in Scheme "B" & made reconnaissance of Scheme "B" & Corps Line. Nos. III & IV Sections carried out Schemes "A" & "B" on the ground. Afternoon devoted to continuation of fatigues; weather mild & camp still very muddy.	

Instructions regarding War Diaries and Intelligence Summaries are contained in F. S. Regs., Part II. and the Staff Manual respectively. Title pages will be prepared in manuscript.

WAR DIARY
or
INTELLIGENCE SUMMARY.
(Erase heading not required.)

(7)

Army Form C. 2118.

Place	Date	Hour	Summary of Events and Information	Remarks and references to Appendices
HEAUDECOURT	25/1/18	–	Inspected No. II Section & found it satisfactory. Nos. I & II carried out defense schemes on the ground. Visited positions of No. IV section in Schemes "B" & Corps Line. Fatigues as usual & programme parades carried out by one section. Reported to D.M.G.O. at Divisional Hq. during afternoon & decided details of defense schemes etc. Lt. Leslie proceeded to PERONNE to attend course in communication by pigeon.	
"	26/1/18	–	Parades as per programme & including one hour's gas drill. Weather mild & misty. Issued Operation order re relief of 64th M.G. Coy. on 27th inst.	APPENDIX
"	27/1/18	–	Morning devoted to church parades followed by preparation for relief. Inspection of socks, feet, iron rations etc. Limbers packed. Sections paraded as per Operation Order & proceeded to Left Sector to relieve 64th Coy. Saw O.C. Lincolns at his Hq. in the line with reference to proposed raid by his Battn. tonight. Decided	

(A7092). Wt. W12839/M1293. 750,000. 1/17. D. D. & L., Ltd. Forms/C.2118/14.

Army Form C. 2118.

Instructions regarding War Diaries and Intelligence Summaries are contained in F. S. Regs., Part II. and the Staff Manual respectively. Title pages will be prepared in manuscript.

WAR DIARY
or
INTELLIGENCE SUMMARY.
(Erase heading not required.)

(18)

Place	Date	Hour	Summary of Events and Information	Remarks and references to Appendices
			details of M.G. support & issued orders accordingly. Reinforcement was cancelled at 4.30pm.	
			Misty day favoured relief which was completed by 6pm.	
			Checked calculations for S.O.S. barrage during the evening. Situation very quiet except for occasional hostile shelling of back areas between 8pm & 10pm. Relief without incident.	
			Supplied O.C. 117th Coy M.G.C. with details of area with view to proposed relief by ~~that unit~~ during next few days.	
HEAUDECOURT	28/1/18	–	Went round all guns in the sector. Decided on work & firing to be done by each section. Found positions on the whole unsatisfactory. Situation very quiet. Trenches in bad condition as a result of recent weather. Arranged for several immediate improvements including provision of A.A. mountings for several guns.	
			Divisional Commander inspected the company transport. He was satisfied, placing it second in the Brigade.	

Instructions regarding War Diaries and Intelligence Summaries are contained in F. S. Regs., Part II. and the Staff Manual respectively. Title pages will be prepared in manuscript.

WAR DIARY
or
INTELLIGENCE SUMMARY.
(*Erase heading not required.*)

(9)

Army Form C. 2118.

Place	Date	Hour	Summary of Events and Information	Remarks and references to Appendices
HEAUDECOURT IN THE LINE	29/1/18	–	Visited all guns with G.S.O.2 21st Division. He expressed satisfaction with his inspection. Situation quiet except for gas shelling by the enemy & counter battery work. Harrassing fire carried out during the night 8000 rds. being fired on various targets. Work on emplacements accelerated by working parties from 64th M.G. Coy. in view of relief by 114th M.G. Coy. on the 31st inst. Lt. Leslie returned from course.	
"	30/1/18	–	Visited sector offices & found everything in order. Work completed on all forward guns & all trench stores overhauled prior to relief. Fatigues to complete rear positions. Bright day with excellent visibility: adverse activity on both sides but otherwise conditions normal. O.C. 114th Coy. reported to make arrangements re relief. Completed these & visited sector with him. Issued Operation Orders for relief on 31st inst. Night quiet except for bombing attacks on back areas. Harrassing fire carried out, 7,000 rds. expended.	APPENDIX.
"	31/1/18	–	Work on area reported complete by 12 noon. Heavy mist all day. Relief by 114th & 228th Coys. carried out & completed by 7.30 p.m. Company in HEAUDECOURT during night. The Coy. has now completed two months without casualties.	

Jas. Chalmers Capt. Comdg. 62nd M.G.C.

(A7092) Wt W12839/M1293 750,000 1/17. D. D. & L., Ltd. Forms/C.2118/14.

Instructions regarding War Diaries and Intelligence Summaries are contained in F. S. Regs., Part II. and the Staff Manual respectively. Title pages will be prepared in manuscript.

WAR DIARY
or
INTELLIGENCE SUMMARY.
(Erase heading not required.)

Army Form C. 2118.

62nd Coy M.G.C. Vol 24

Place	Date	Hour	Summary of Events and Information	Remarks and references to Appendices
HEAUDECOURT	1/2/18	-	Devoted day to cleaning guns, stores, equipment etc. & packing limbers in preparation for move on 2nd inst. Issued orders for move. Lt. [illegible] & 5 O.R. proceeded as advance party to HAUT ALLAINES to take over camp. Weather conditions excellent.	
	2/2/18	-	Paraded 10.45am. & marched out at 11am. Company well turned out & in excellent spirits. Marched via WARAMONT, AIZECOURT LE BAS, AIZECOURT LE HAUT to HAUT ALLAINES arriving at 2.30pm. Roads were very bad but there was no difficulty with feet. Found good accomodation waiting, but the camp generally was very dirty having been vacated by Indian Labour Corps. Advance party has cleaned billets sufficiently for men to settle down. [illegible] for all ranks. Cover secured for all animals. Submitted programme for following week.	APPENDIX "A"
HAUT ALLAINES	3/2/18	-	Church Parades & camp fatigues.	
"	4/2/18	-	Parades as per programme. Found equipment generally well up to date & in good order. N.C.O's showed an intelligent grasp of the compass at the afternoon class conducted by Lt. LESLIE. Lecture by O.C. 1st M.M.G. Battery on M.Gs. as A.A. weapons.	

(A7092). Wt W12839/M1293 75,000 1/17. D. D. & L., Ltd. Forms/C.2118/14.

Instructions regarding War Diaries and Intelligence Summaries are contained in F. S. Regs., Part II. and the Staff Manual respectively. Title pages will be prepared in manuscript.

WAR DIARY
or
INTELLIGENCE SUMMARY.
(Erase heading not required.)

Army Form C. 2118.

(2)

Place	Date	Hour	Summary of Events and Information	Remarks and references to Appendices
HAUT ALLAINES	5/2/18	-	Parades as per programme. Found T.O.E.T. very much in need of practice, men were slow + inaccurate. Gun carriages thoroughly cleaned during the afternoon. Officers' class in barrage showed that all officers had an excellent theoretical knowledge of the work but that the new officers lacked experience in the actual practice of M.G. barrages. 2/Lt. RUDKIN proceeded to U.K. on leave.	
"	6/2/18	-	Parades as per programme. All ranks showed much improvement noticeable in squad drill + T.O.E.T. N.C.O's class continued under Lt LESLIE. The new Sergeants seem intelligent + well trained, though in two cases they lack command on parade. 2/Lt. JACKS proceeded to PERONNE on [illegible] course. Lecture by Divisional Commander on the work of the Division.	
"	7/2/18	-	Parades continued. All fighting limbers washed during afternoon. Officers class in barrage continued, the use of charts being dealt with. 2/Lt. EDMUNDSON proceeded to BOULOGNE to attend demonstration in camouflage + other R.E. work.	

Instructions regarding War Diaries and Intelligence Summaries are contained in F. S. Regs., Part II. and the Staff Manual respectively. Title pages will be prepared in manuscript.

WAR DIARY
or
INTELLIGENCE SUMMARY.
(Erase heading not required.)

Army Form C. 2118.

(3)

Place	Date	Hour	Summary of Events and Information	Remarks and references to Appendices
HAUT ALLAINES	8/2/18	–	Parades as per programme. Inspections very satisfactory: [illegible] [illegible] marked improvement in squad drill, saluting & I.O.M.G.	
"	9/2/18	–	I.O.M.G. competition gave very mixed results. Belt filling by machine was very unsatisfactory but filling by hand gave good results. Stoppages were fair. Great progress was shown in mounting gun, loading etc. The competition was keenly contested; No. III Section won easily on total points.	
"	10/2/18	–	Church parades for all denominations. O.C. Coy attended conference at Div. HQ. where Battn. scheme for M.G. Coys was explained by Major Settle. Issued new training programme.	APPENDIX "B"
"	11/2/18		Parades as per programme. Coy. Drill Parade was fair. Barrage drill needs much practice. Conference of officers at 11 am. discussing tactical schemes, barrage drill & training for the week. Company worked on football ground during afternoon. C.S.M. instructed N.C.Os in duties & drill. No. 1 Section Officer made reconnaissance of night duties of Divisional front.	

(A7092) Wt W12839/M1293 750,000 1/17. D. D. & L., Ltd. Forms/C.2118/14.

Instructions regarding War Diaries and Intelligence Summaries are contained in F. S. Regs., Part II. and the Staff Manual respectively. Title pages will be prepared in manuscript.

WAR DIARY
or
INTELLIGENCE SUMMARY.
(Erase heading not required.)

(4)

Army Form C. 2118.

Place	Date	Hour	Summary of Events and Information	Remarks and references to Appendices
HAUT ALLAINES	12/2/18	–	Company drill considerably improved. Section cannot yet surpass [illegible] exercises. The inexperience of many of the men is apparent. Water bearing supply had not received sufficient attention & surprise situations were weakly dealt with. Much training is required in the open. Five more officers made reconnaissance of Br. Div. sector.	
"	13/2/18	–	Programme interrupted to allow for bathing & gas parades at MOISLAINS. Half coy bathed at 9am, half at 10.30am. Half coy had box respirators tested in gas chamber at MOISLAINS at 11am & half coy at 12 noon. Afternoon devoted to cleaning billets & packing in readiness for moving on following day. Coy. concert in Church Army Hut during the evening. All ranks in excellent spirits.	
"	14/2/18	–	Prepared to move to TINCOURT. Paraded at 2.15pm & marched out at 2.30pm, arriving TINCOURT at 4.45pm. Advance party had preceded coy & had tea waiting the men. Billets very good all ranks having beds. [illegible] covered lines available for transport.	

(A7092). Wt. W12839/M1293. 75 ,0 0. 1/17. D. D. & L., Ltd. Forms/C.2118/14.

WAR DIARY
or
INTELLIGENCE SUMMARY.
(Erase heading not required.)

(5)

Army Form C. 2118.

Instructions regarding War Diaries and Intelligence Summaries are contained in F. S. Regs., Part II. and the Staff Manual respectively. Title pages will be prepared in manuscript.

Place	Date	Hour	Summary of Events and Information	Remarks and references to Appendices
TINCOURT	15/2/18	–	Transport proceeded to SAULCOURT where covered standings were available. [illegible] [illegible] showed improvement but [illegible] of [illegible] [illegible] [illegible]. Camp thoroughly cleaned during afternoon. Officers [illegible] class by O.C. Coy.	
"	16/2/18	–	Coy drill was [illegible] – men [illegible] too cold. [illegible] [illegible]. Officers class revised yesterday's work. Men devoted [illegible] morning to cleaning [illegible] of equipment & gun belts. Semi final of section [illegible]-a-side football competition played in afternoon. Conference with D.M.G.C. at HQ 237th Coy at 6 p.m. General situation discussed & the necessary action to meet it decided. Lt. SHEPHERD proceeded on leave.	
"	17/2/18	–	Church parades for all denominations. Fighting limbers brought down from SAULCOURT & loaded ready to move if required. Rugby match v 64th Coy. during afternoon. Programme for ensuing week issued.	APPENDIX "C".
"	18/2/18	–	Parades as per programme. Officers conference at 11 a.m. Points brought out at D.M.G.C.'s conference on Saturday discussed. Made reconnaissance during afternoon with a view to defence of vicinity of billets in accordance with instructions received.	

(A7092). Wt W12839/M1293 75 ,0 o. 1/17. D. D. & L., Ltd. Forms/C.2118/14.

Army Form C. 2118.

Instructions regarding War Diaries and Intelligence Summaries are contained in F. S. Regs., Part II. and the Staff Manual respectively. Title pages will be prepared in manuscript.

WAR DIARY
or
INTELLIGENCE SUMMARY.
(Erase heading not required.)

Place	Date	Hour	Summary of Events and Information	Remarks and references to Appendices
			Decided on dispositions & reported accordingly. Supplied two A.A. M.G. detachments for defence of Division H.Q. Final of inter section football competition played during the afternoon.	
			Fatigue of 2 N.C.O. & 20 men supplied to Area Commandant.	
TINCOURT	19/2/18	–	Parades as per programme. Ammunition supply reports. Fire control practices on Tactical schemes. Lecture "Troops in Bourlon Wood during 1917". Attended conference at H.Q. 23rd Coy. at 9.30 am & obtained general idea of new defence scheme. Troops attended concert given by 237 M.G. Coy. in the Theatre TINCOURT during the evening. 2/Lt [illegible] accidentally injured; Lt. Stephenson acting in his place.	
"	20/2/18	–	Inspected Coy. Transport H.Qs. & No. 2 Section excellently turned out. Nos. I & IV Sections fair & No. III bad. Visiting line carried out by half companies [illegible] proper manner. Reconnaissance of northern area including FINS, GOUZEAUCOURT, REVELON RIDGE, CHAPEL HILL & SAULCOURT area in accordance with orders re new defence scheme. Football match v 110th M.G. Coy. during afternoon.	

Instructions regarding War Diaries and Intelligence Summaries are contained in F. S. Regs., Part II. and the Staff Manual respectively. Title pages will be prepared in manuscript.

WAR DIARY
or
INTELLIGENCE SUMMARY.
(Erase heading not required.)

Army Form C. 2118.

(7)

Place	Date	Hour	Summary of Events and Information	Remarks and references to Appendices
Tincourt	21/2/18	–	Programme to admit of baths for all ranks. Adjusted all parades accordingly. Lt. Leslie + Lt. Jack made reconnaissance of forward area in compliance with Divisional Defence Scheme. O.C. Coy. made reconnaissance of left area in view of orders received as to action of Coy. in case of enemy attack. Visited entraining + detraining points, lines of approach + northern Corps boundary. Lt. Watson to Pigeon Course.	
"	22/2/18	–	Made reconnaissance of Rt. Bge area of 16th Div. with a view to relief. Visited all guns with D.M.G.C. Section Officers + Section Sgts. made reconnaissance in accordance with Defence Scheme. Coy. on route march from 9 am to 12.30 pm. Section practices during afternoon.	
"	23/2/18	–	C. of E. Battn. Church Parade. 1 Off. 1 Sgt. 1 Cpl. + 12 men per section on parade. Special services for R.Co. + Presbyterians. D.M.G.C. interviewed all Sgts + decorated ranks in the Coy.	

Instructions regarding War Diaries and Intelligence Summaries are contained in F. S. Regs., Part II. and the Staff Manual respectively. Title pages will be prepared in manuscript.

WAR DIARY
or
INTELLIGENCE SUMMARY.
(*Erase heading not required.*)

Army Form C. 2118.

Place	Date	Hour	Summary of Events and Information	Remarks and references to Appendices
TINCOURT	24/2/18	–	Capt Chalmers went to Div to act as 2nd in Command of Batt while Capt Borthwick proceeds on leave. Lieut W.S. [illegible] took over Command of the Company.	
"	25/2/18	–	The four Companies assembled with [illegible] and were addressed by Major [illegible] on [illegible] of [illegible] of the Batt. [illegible] at 11.30 am. The shooting on range was [illegible] [illegible] and the [illegible] [illegible] officers & NCOs of the Companies [illegible] Remainder of Coy engaged in cleaning.	
"	26/2/18	–	Inspection of the Batt by the G.O.C. 21 Division. He complimented the Company and said the turn-out was "very creditable". Made reconnaissance of the Right Brigade Front of the 16th Division in the afternoon. Company packing limbers for [illegible]	
RONSSOY	27/2/18	–	entrained at Tincourt at 4.15 pm and detrained at St Emilie at 5 pm. Relief of 49 M.G. Coy complete by 9 pm. HQ at St Emilie about 4 kilometres from the line	
"	28/2/18	–	Left HQ 9 am and returned at 12.05 pm. During that time visit 13 gun positions and all four section officers. Dispositions were No 3 Sect on right No 2 in Centre No 1 Sec on left, No 4, Rear Centre	[illegible] 62 M.G.C

(A7092). Wt W12839/M1293. 75,000. 1/17. D. D. & L., Ltd. Forms/C.2118/14.

SECRET.

OO No. J. 30.

Map Ref. Villers Guislain 57c S.E. 4.

(1) The Coy will be relieved in the line by 117 M.G. Coy. & 228 M.G. Coy on the 31st inst.

(2) 228 M.G. Coy will relieve L.17, L.18, L.19 & L.20 under arrangements to be notified later

(3) 117 M.G. Coy will relieve the Right Forward & the Left Forward Groups complete. One Section 117 Coy will relieve L.15, L.9, L.11 & L.12.

(4) Guides from L.15, L.9, L.11 & L.12 will be at Railton Cross Roads W.22.b.90/95 at 1.30 pm on the 31st inst where they will meet their relieving teams.

(5) Guides from all guns in Right & Left Forward Groups will be at Railton Cross Roads at 4.30 pm on the 31st inst.

(6) Lt. S. Edmundson will be in charge of the guides mentioned in para 4; the relieving Section Officer will take over his headquarters.

Lt. Rudkin will be in charge of guides mentioned in para 5.

(7) Tripods, belt boxes, reserve SAA & all trench stores will be handed over & receipts obtained, these being rendered to Orderly Room on return

(5)

to Henencourt.

(8) Range cards, orders, SOS lines etc will be carefully handed over.

(9) Relief complete will be reported to Coy. Hdqr. HQ

(10) Officer i/c Transport will arrange for one limber to be at each of the Forward Section HQ at 5.30 pm & for one limber to be at W.18.c.7.5 at 2 pm. Having picked up guns etc. from L.11 & L.12 the last mentioned limber will report at W.23.b.17.0 to pick up guns from L.9 & L.15.

(11) On relief Sections will return to billets at Henencourt.

(12) Positions, dugouts, trenches etc. will be left scrupulously clean, & every facility will be given to the relieving units.

(Sd) Jas Chalmers Capt

Comdg. 62 MG Coy

30/1/18.

62 Machine Gun Coy.

SECRET.

Operation Orders No. 26.

Copy No. 11

Ref Map Sheet – VILLERS GUISLAIN, 57C. S.E. 4

1. The Coy. will relieve 64 Coy. in the line during the afternoon of 27.1.18.

2. The Coy. Rear H.Q. and Transport Lines will remain in their present positions at HEUDECOURT.

3. Coy. Advanced H.Q. will open at 5 p.m. in the Railway Cutting at approximately W23.a.8.1.

4. Nos. 1, 2 and 4 Sections will parade at 2.15 p.m. and will move off by Sections at five minutes interval; commencing at 2.45 p.m. Necessary transport will be at Coy. H.Q. at 2 p.m. No 3 Section will parade at 3.15 p.m. and will move off at 3.45 p.m. Requisite transport will be at Coy. H.Q. at 3 p.m. Teams will consist of at least 1 N.C.O. and 4 men.

5. The guns will be divided into 4 Groups, viz:–
   (a) Right forward
   (b) Right rear
   (c) Left forward
   (d) Left rear.

6. (a) No. 3 Section under Lieut. Watson will relieve the positions of the Right forward group.
   (b) No. 4 Section under 2/Lieut. Raudkin will relieve the Right rear group.
   (c) No. 1 Section under Lieut. Stephenson will relieve the Left forward group.
   (d) No 2 Section under 2/Lieut. Edmundson will relieve the Left rear group.

7. Guides for No. 4 Section will be at Coy. Advanced H.Q. at 3.30 p.m. and guides for Nos. 1 and 2 Sections at L19 gun position at 3.30 p.m. (L4 of Left forward group will not be relieved until 5.30 p.m.
   Guides for No 3 Section will be at L19 position at 4.30 p.m.

8. All S.O.S. and battle lines will be taken over and carefully checked. Tripods, belt boxes, S.A.A. etc will be taken over from 64 Coy.
   All trench stores will be taken over and copies of the receipts given sent to Coy. Advanced H.Q.

9. "Relief complete" will be reported by runner to Coy. Advanced H.Q.

10. Divisional Orders issued herewith will supersede Coy. Orders. Sentries 'information sheets' are also issued. These will be filled up by Section Officers and one copy kept at each gun.

11. The unexpended portion of rations for the 27th inst. will be carried on the man, and the whole of the rations for the 28th inst.
12. The rations will leave Coy. Stores at 3.30 p.m. each day
13. Each section will take up eight petrol tins of water, and on subsequent days full tins of water will only be given on receiving a corresponding number of empty ones.
14. Section Officers will take a supply of glycerine and whale oil into the line.
15 Acknowledge.

26 1. 18

J Boswell
Lieut. & Adjt.
62nd Machine Gun Coy.

Distribution.

Copy No. 1 .. D.M.G.O.
" " 2 .. 62nd Inf. Bde
" " 3-6 .. Section Officers
" " 7 .. O.C. Lair
" " 8 .. Transport Officer
" " 9 .. C.O.
" " 10 .. File
" " 11 & 12 .. War Diary.

62 Machine Gun Coy.
Operation Order No. S.21.

SECRET.
Copy No. 8
War Diary

Ref Map Sheet 57c. S.E.4

With reference to 21st Divisional Defence Schemes "A" "B" & "C", existing orders re dispositions & action of the Coy. are hereby cancelled, and the following substituted :-

SCHEME "A". On receipt of orders to carry out Scheme "A" Sections will move as follows:-

No. 3 Section to positions at

W.23 a. 45.55 (approx.) firing 7° M (approx.)
" 70.60 " " 132° "
" b. 10.20 " " 182° "
20.10 " " 15° "

No. 2 Section to positions at

W.23.c. 75.45 (approx.) firing 157° M (approx.)
" 90.25 " " 182° "
W.29.b. 10.90 " " 142° "
" 20.75 " " 157° "

Nos. 1 & 4 Sections to reserve assembly positions in W.23.c.

Coy H.Q. will be at W. 29.c. 70.80.

SCHEME "B". On receipt of orders to carry out Scheme "B", Sections will move as follows:-

No. 3 Section to positions at

W.23.b. 10.20 (approx.) firing 182° M (approx.)
" 20.10 " " 15° "
" c. 75.45 " " 157° "
" 90.25 " " 182° "

No. 1 Section to positions at

W.29.b. 25.40 (approx.) firing 112° M (approx.)
" a. 40.50 " " 350° "
W.28.c. 20.70 " " 135° "
W.22.d. 40.25 " " 5° "

No. 4 Section to positions at

W.22.c. 30.10 (approx.) firing 135° M (approx.)
W.22.c. 10.40 " " 7° "
W.21.d. 80.10 " " 167° "
W.21.b. 10.20 " " 157° "

No. 2 Section to reserve assembly positions in W.28.a.

Coy. H.Q. will be at W.29.c. 70.80.

SCHEME "C". On receipt of orders to carry out Scheme "C" the Coy. will move to reserve assembly position in E 22 b.

CORPS LINE SCHEME. On receipt of orders to occupy the Corps Line guns will be disposed as follows

3 guns of No 3 Section to positions at
W. 16. d. 75.40 (approx) firing 112° M (approx)
W 16 d. 85.25 " " 67° "
W. 16 d. 80.00 " " 82° "

3 guns of No 2 Section to positions at
W. 22. b. 10.30 (approx) firing 80° M (approx.)
W 22 d. 20.95 " " 90° "
" 05.90 " " 212° "

4 guns of No 1 Section to positions at
W 22 c. 40.00 (approx.) firing 72° M (approx)
W 28 a. 40.90 " " 72° "
" 20.75 " " 190° "
" 15.50 " " 190° "

1 gun of No 2 Section under Section Sergeant to
W. 27. d. 80.00 (approx.) firing 70° M (approx)
& the remaining guns of the Coy.
Coy. H.Q. will remain in HEUDECOURT pending further orders.

[illegible] Capt.
Comdg 62 Machine Gun Coy.

21.1.18

DISTRIBUTION.
Copy No 1 .. DMGO.
" 2 .. OC. Coy.
" 3 .. OC. No 1 Section.
" 4 .. OC. No 2 "
" 5 .. OC No 3 "
" 6 .. OC. No 4
" 7+8 .. War Diary.

War Diary

62nd Machine Gun Coy O.O. 301.

SECRET.

18.1.18.

VILLERS GUISLAIN 57c. S.E.4. Ed. 3A.

(1) The Coy will be relieved by 64 M.G. Coy. on 19-1-18 & will proceed to billets in HEUDECOURT.

(2) 1 Guide per team for Right Rear Group will be at Section HQ at W 23.b. 70.00 at 2.30 pm. 1 Guide per team for the 3 remaining Groups will be at L.19 position in W.18.c 05.20 at 2-30 pm

(3) The following guns will be relieved after dusk under orders to be issued by 62 Coy to Guides – L.1, L.4. If front line trench is impassable, this will apply to L.2, L.3.

(4) Certificates of cleanliness of dugouts, emplacements and latrines will be obtained from Section Officers of 64 Coy & sent to Coy HQ in Railway Cutting upon completion of relief.

(5) All S.O.S. lines and battle lines will be carefully handed over, and explained to relieving Coy Officers.

(6) All trench stores will be carefully handed over & receipts obtained. Belt boxes & tripods will not be handed over.

(7) Programmes of work to be done will be handed over by Section Officers to relieving Officers. Details of work in progress will be very carefully explained.

(8) Maps will be handed over.

(9) All alternative emplacements will be shown to relieving Officers.

(10) Breakfast & tea rations only will be sent up for the 19th. Second in Command will make arrangements for dinner to be served to Sections upon arrival at HEUDECOURT.

(11) Necessary transport for relief will be at Section HQ by 3 pm.

(12) Receipts for trench stores will be handed in to Coy Orderly Room.

(13) Relief complete to be reported to Coy HQ in Railway.

(14) ACKNOWLEDGE.

W H Kfthenson
Lieut & Adjt
62 Machine Gun Coy.

(2)

12. The unexpired portion of rations for the 11th inst. will be carried on the man and the whole of the rations for the 12th inst. if they arrive in time will be taken into the line.

If the latter rations do not arrive in time they will be sent to Coy. Advanced H.Q. on mules and will be met there by guides from each section. The guides will show the transport drivers to what point the rations for subsequent days will be brought.

13. The rations will leave Coy. Stores at 3.30 p.m. each day.

14. Each section will take up eight petrol tins of water, and on subsequent days full tins of water will only be given on receiving a corresponding number of empty ones.

15. Section Officers will take a supply of glycerine and whale-oil into the line.

16. Acknowledge.

W.H. Stephenson

Lieut. and A/Adjt.
62nd Machine Gun Coy.

Distribution.

Copy No. 1 .. D.M.G.O.
" 2 .. 62 Inf. Bde.
" 3–6 .. Section Officers.
" 7 .. O.C. Lalr
" 8 .. Transport Officer
" 9 .. C.O.
" 10 .. File
" 11 & 12 .. War Diary.

[illegible] Gun Coy. [illegible] SECRET.
Operation Order No. 101. Copy No.

1. The Company will relieve 64 Coy. in the line during the afternoon of 11. 11. 1918.

2. The Coy. Rear H.Q. and Transport Lines will remain in their present position at HEUDECOURT.

3. Coy. Advanced H.Q. will open at 3 pm in the Railway cutting at approximately W.13.a.8.4, map sheet 57c. S.E.

4. The Coy will parade at 1 pm. and will move off by Section at 1.30 pm with five minutes interval between Sections. Necessary transport will be at Coy. Stores at 12.45 pm. Teams will consist of at least, a N.C.O. and 4 men.

5. The guns will be divided into 4 groups, viz:-
(a) Right Forward.
(b) Right Rear
(c) Left Forward
(d) Left Rear.

6. (a) No. 2 Section under 2/Lieut. S. Edmondson will relieve the positions of the Right Forward Group.
(b) No. 3 Section under 2/Lieut. G. W. Jack will relieve the Right Rear Group.
(c) No. 4 Section under 2/Lieut G. H. Ruskin will relieve the Left Forward Group.
(d) No. 1 Section under 2/Lieut. C. H. R. Shepherd will relieve the Left Rear Group.

7. All guns will be relieved by day except L1 in the Right Forward Group and L4, 5 and 6 in the Left Forward Group. These guns will be relieved according to instructions issued to the guides by O.C. 64 Coy.

8. Guides for No. 3 Section will be at Coy. Advanced H.Q at 2.30 pm. and guides for the other 3 Sections at L19 gun position at 2.30 p.m.

9. One team of No. 3 Section will remain at Coy. Advanced H.Q. in reserve.

10. All S.O.S. and battle lines will be taken over and carefully checked. Tripods, belt boxes, S.A.A. etc: will be taken over from 64 Coy. with the exception of No. 1 Section which will take its compliment of belt boxes into the line.
All trench-stores will be taken over and copies of the receipts given sent to Coy. Advanced H.Q.
"Relief complete" will be reported by runner to Coy. Advanced H.Q.

(3)

SAULCOURT. A representative will report at Reserve Brigade HQ at [illegible] would be in [illegible] scheme B No 2 Section reserve at HEUDECOURT.

J. Boswell
Lieut Col
62nd Machine Gun Coy

Distribution

1 – 3 .. .. War Diary & File.
4 .. .. OC
5 – 8 .. .. Section Officers.
9 .. .. Adjutant
10 T.O.
11 .. .. D.M.G.O
12 .. .. 62nd Inf. Bde.

(2)

[illegible] of Company in case of Scheme "B"

No 3 Section will take up positions:–

W 23 b 15.40. 85°
W 23 c 80.65. 45°
W 23 c 95.50 75°
W 29 b 30.60 20°

No. 1 Section will take up positions as follows:–

W 22 c. 45.45 350°
W 29 a. 50.70 330°
W 28 c. 20.90 45°
W 28 a. 50.20 25°

No. 4 Section.

W 21 b 05.40 50°
W 21 d. 80.90 60°
W 22 c 15.65 350°
W 22 c. 80.40 40°

Each section will in turn practice taking up its positions as if the schemes were actually in operation. Sections will be detailed in daily orders. (No 3 Section 8/1/18)

Officers commanding sections will treat the scheme as a means of training in [illegible] use of cover etc.

Each team will be shown its position on the ground, [illegible] [illegible], H.Q., Section H.Q. and so on.

If conditions are favourable, Section Officers will carry out [illegible] the action [illegible] actually in action, supply of ammunition to the guns [illegible] etc.

It must be impressed [illegible] that the scheme may sometime become real and each man must know exactly what he has to do.

Section Officers will report to Coy. H.Q. on [illegible] the positions of their proposed H.Q.

[illegible] of Transport, [illegible] and ammunition [illegible] will be [illegible].

In case of Scheme C (attack on Right Divisional Flank) [illegible] Brigade will form a defensive flank facing South East. General line, strong point at [illegible] along [illegible] – [illegible] [illegible].

Company will move to assembly position [illegible] E.9.c. [illegible]

Operation Orders for 62nd M.G. Company War Diary in reserve in case of enemy break-through on left of Divisional front (Schemes A & B)

Ref Map Sheet VILLERS GUISLAIN.

General Scheme – Scheme A. Reserve Brigade will hold the ground between PEIZIERE and REVELON FARM as a support to the Brown line running through W 18. b & d. General line will be the railway from W20 b 88 to W23. a 9.1. Support line from strong point at W. 30. b. 54. north westwards to the spur which runs through W 23 c & d

Scheme B. Reserve Brigade will form a defensive flank pivoting on EPEHY PEIZIERE facing North-east. General line as in scheme A, on right and on left along the high ground in W 21 and W 22.

Action of the Company. The Company will move under orders issued by B.G.C. Left Brigade to assembly positions in W 23 c (Nos. 2 & 3 Sections) and near cross roads in W 28. b (Nos. 1 & 4 Sections)

O.C. will proceed to Right Reserve Battalion H.Q. near W. 30. c. 9.8 and await orders for scheme to come into force

When guns are in positions he will move to H.Q. near Reserve Brigade H.Q. in E 10 a 1.3.

Route of approach to assembly positions will be along road running through W 21 b, 22 c, and 28 b.

Disposition of Company in case of Scheme A.

No. 3 Section Gun positions:-

Position — Approx. direction of fire T.B.

W. 23 a. 45 72.
W. 23. b. 15. 40.
W. 23. b. 25. 25.
W. 23 c. 80. 65.

345°
85°
10°
45°

No. 2 Section Gun positions:-

W 23 c. 95 80.
W 23 d. 10 10.
W 29 b. 15 85.
W 30 c. 70 90.

75°
40°
40°
350°

Nos. 1 and 4 Sections in Reserve in assembly positions.

62nd Company Machine Gun Corps — SECRET

Operation Orders 1.1.

Villers Guislain 57c. S.E. 4 Edn 3d.

1) The Company will be relieved by 64 M. G. Coy on 3/1/18 and will proceed to billets in HEUDECOURT.

2) Guides 1 guide per team for Right Rear Group will be at Section H.Q. at W 23 b 90.10 at 2.30 p.m. 1 guide per team for Right Forward Group and two left groups will be at L 19 position in W 18. c. 05.20 at 2.30 p.m.

3) The following guns will be relieved after dusk under orders to be issued by O.C. 62 Company to guides. L1, L4, & L6.

4) Certificates re cleanliness of shelters, emplacements, latrines, etc: will be obtained from Section Officers of 64 Coy and sent to Coy. H.Q. in Railway Cutting upon completion of relief.

5) All S.O.S. and battle lines will be carefully handed over and explained to relieving company officers.

6) Everything except guns and spare parts will be handed over and receipts obtained.

7) Programmes of work to be done will be handed by Section Officers to relieving officers. Details of work in progress will be very carefully explained.

8) Maps etc. will be handed over.

9) Separate orders re belt boxes of Right Rear Group will be given to officer concerned.

10) Breakfast and tea rations only will be sent up on the 3rd. The Second in Command will make arrangements for dinner to be served to sections upon arrival at HEUDECOURT.

11) Necessary transport for relief will be at Section H.Q. by 3 P.M.

12) Receipts for trench stores etc: to be handed in to Coy. Orderly Room.

13) "Relief complete" to be reported to Coy. H.Q. in Railway Cutting.

14) Acknowledge.

1/1/18.

[illegible]
Lieut. & A/Adjt
62nd Machine Gun Coy.

62 Machine Gun Coy.

Programme of Work for backward men and reinforcements.

20th Sunday. Baths and general cleaning.
21st Monday. Cleaning gun gear + limbers.
All necessary kit + equipment inspections.

Date.	9-9.30 a.m.	9.45 am.	10-10.30 am	10.30-11 am	11.15-11.45 am	11.45am-12.15 pm	12.15-12.45 pm
22nd	Physical Training	Section Inspection	Gun Drill	Mechanism	Revolver Drill	Lecture on Trench Duties	Coy. Drill
23rd			Gun Drill	Immediate Action	Stoppages	Lecture on Revolvers	Revolver Drill
24th			Belt filling and instruction on belt filling machine			Points b. d. a.	Coy. Drill
25th			Gun Drill	Immediate Action	Stoppages	Lecture on Camouflaging	Revolver Drill
26th			Building isolated M. G. positions.				Coy. Drill

19/1/18. Training to take place at HBUDECOURT.

W.S.G. Freeman

[illegible] for O.C.
62 Machine Gun Coy.

62 Machine Gun Coy.

Programme of Work for No 1. men showing ability + junior N C O's

20th Sunday. Baths + general cleaning

21st Monday. Cleaning of gun gear + limbers. All necessary kit + equipment inspections.

Date	9 - 9.30 am	9.45 am	10 - 10.30 am	10.30 - 11 am	11.15 - 11.45 am	11.45 am - 12.15 pm	12.15 - 12.45 pm	Remarks
22nd	Physical Training	Inspection	Gun Drill	Mechanism	Immediate Action	Lecture on Lunch Duties	Company Drill	Junior NCO's at disposal of C.S.M from 12.15 - 12.45 pm.
23rd			Mechanism	Use of dials + chronometer	Prolonged Stoppages	Map Reading	Revolver Drill	Inspection by O.C.
24th			Belt filling + instruction on belt filling machine			Points L. d. a.	Company Drill	Junior NCO's at disposal of CSM from 12.15 - 12.45 pm
25th			Compass	Lectures on Indirect Fire Rules for Indirect Fire, etc.			Barrage Drill	Inspection by 2nd in Command
26th			Building isolated M.G. positions				Company Drill	Junior NCO's at disposal of CSM from 12.15 - 12.45 pm
27th			Preparing for line and relief					

By 6 pm 20/1/18 Section Officers will have divided their Sections into Classes as above. They will also render to Orderly Room by same time the names of Sergeants + Corporals to act as Instructors, stating whether for Advanced or Reinforcement Class.

19-1-18.

Training to take place at HEUDECOURT.

[illegible] for a/Capt.
62 Machine Gun Coy

www.ingramcontent.com/pod-product-compliance
Lightning Source LLC
Chambersburg PA
CBHW081529160426
43191CB00011B/1714

* 9 7 8 1 4 7 4 5 1 2 2 2 0 *